"每天读一点英文"
Everyday English Snack
中英双语+MP3

每天读一点英文
Everyday English Snack

那些妙趣横生的故事
Those witty stories

章华◎编译

与美国人同步阅读的英语丛书
—美国英语教师协会推荐—

时代文艺出版社

图书在版编目（CIP）数据

那些妙趣横生的故事：英汉对照／章华编译．—长春：时代文艺出版社，2010.1

（每天读一点英文）

ISBN 978-7-5387-2974-0

Ⅰ．那…　Ⅱ．章…　Ⅲ．①英语—汉语—对照读物

②故事—作品集—世界　Ⅳ．H319.4：I

中国版本图书馆CIP数据核字（2010）第016627号

出 品 人　张四季

责任编辑　苗欣宇　付　娜

策 划 人　博集天卷·辛　艳

技术设计　杨俊红

装帧设计　张丽娜　李　洁

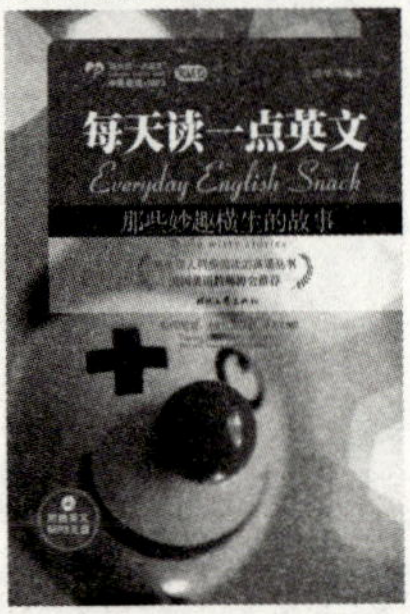

那些妙趣横生的故事

章　华　编译

出版发行／时代文艺出版社

地址／长春市泰来街1825号　时代文艺出版社　邮编／130062

总编办／0431-86012927　发行科／0431-86012939

网址／www.shidaichina.com

印刷／北京嘉业印刷厂

开本／880×1230毫米　1/32　字数／200千字　印张／8

版次／2010年6月第1版　印次／2012年1月第3次印刷　定价／26.80元

目录
Contents

Those Witty Stories

那些妙趣横生的故事

目录
Contents

Those Witty Stories
那些妙趣横生的故事

目录

Contents

If life were like a computer
假如生活是一台电脑

You are too late

on a bus a man discovered a pickpocket's hand thrust into his pocket.

"sorry," he said to the **pickpocket**, "you are too late. My wife did it before you."

你太晚了

在公共汽车上，有个人发现小偷把手伸到了他的口袋里。

"对不起，"他对小偷说，"你太晚了，我妻子在你之前就做过同样的事情了。"

★★★★★

It was the Christmas season and the judge was in a merry mood as he asked the prisoner, "What is your offense?"

"I did my Christmas shopping early this year," cried the prisoner.

"There's nothing wrong with that," said the Judge. "How early were you doing this shopping?"

"Before the store opened," answered the prisoner.

圣诞佳节到来，法官心情愉悦地问犯人："你做了什么坏事啊？"
"我今年圣诞节购物早了些。"犯人回答。
"这么做没错啊"，法官说："到底多早之前啊？"
"商店开门之前。"犯人答道。

★★★★★

Problem with gas

A little old lady goes to the doctor and says, "Doctor, I have this problem with gas, but it doesn't really bother me too much. They never **smell** and are always **silent**. **As a matter of fact**, I've farted at least 20 times since I've been here in your office. You didn't know I was farting because they don't smell and are silent." The doctor says, "I see. Here's a **prescription**. Take these pills 3 times a day for seven days and come back to see me next week." The next week the lady goes back. "Doctor," she says, "I don't know what the hell you gave me, but now my farts ... although still silent... **stink** terribly." The doctor says, "Good! **Now that** we've **cleared up** your sinuses, let's start working on your hearing."

放屁的问题

有位小老太太去看医生，她对医生说："医生，我有爱放屁的毛病。其实也不是大问题，因为我放屁不臭而且没声音。事实上，自从我进了你办公室后，已经放了至少20个屁了，但是你并不知道对吧，因为我的屁不臭，而且还没声音。"医生说："好的，我明白了。吃这个药片，一天三次连续吃七天，下星期你再来。"一个星期后，老太太来了，"医生，你到底给的我什么药，现在我放屁还是没声音，但是怎么这么臭！"医生说："太好了！既然你的嗅觉正常了，我们开始治听觉吧。"

★★★★★

If life were like a computer

You could add/remove someone in your life using the **control panel**. You could put your kids in the **recycle** bin and restore them when you feel like it! You could improve your appearance by adjusting the **display** settings. You could turn off the speakers when life gets too noisy. You could click on "find" (Ctrl，F) to recover your lost remote control and car keys. To get your daily exercise，just click on "run" ! If you **mess up** your life，you could always press "Ctrl，Alt，Delete" and start all over!

假如生活是一台电脑

你可以通过控制面板增加或者删除一些人；可以把孩子放进回收站，然后在你喜欢的时候再还原；可以通过调整显示器的设置让外表更好看；可以在吵闹的时候关掉音箱；可以点击"搜索"找到丢失了的遥控器和车钥匙；锻炼身体的时候，点击"运行"。要是你的生活一团糟，同时按下"ctrl，alt，delete"键，一切就会重新开始。

实战提升
Practising & Exercise

单词 & 词组

pickpocket ['pikˌpɔkit] *n.* 扒手，小偷
smell [smel] *n.* 有难闻的气味；气味，臭味；嗅觉
silent ['sailənt] *adj.* 寂静的，沉默的
as a matter of fact 事实上，其实
prescription [pri'skripʃən] *n.* 药方，处方
stink [stiŋk] *v.* 散发出恶臭，发臭味
now that 既然
clear up 打扫干净；治疗，治愈；处理
control panel 控制面板
recycle ['riː'saikl] *v.* 使再循环，反复应用
display [di'splei] *n.* 显示，展示
mess up 搞糟，陷入困境

知道不知道

英文的放屁有很多种说法，比较通俗的说法有 fart，可用作不及物动词和名词。如果想文雅一点，比如有的小朋友喜欢把“放屁”说成“排气”，那么英语里就可以说 break wind，或者 cut the cheese。此外，比较正式的用法还有 expel gas ，pass gas 等。

This is no time to be superstitious!
都什么时候了，还这么迷信！

Much worse

Policeman：Why didn't you shout for help when you were **robbed of** your watch？

Man：If I had opened my mouth，they'd have found my four gold teeth. That would be much worse.

那就更糟了

警察：有人抢你的手表时，你为什么不呼救呢?

男子：要是我张口的话，他们就会发现我的四颗金牙。那就更糟了。

★★★★★

Psychiatrist

Jerry went to a psychiatrist. "Doc," he said，"I've got trouble. Every time I get into bed，I think there's somebody under it. I'm going crazy!" "Just put yourself in my hands for one year," said the **shrink**. "Come to me three times a week，and I'll cure your fears." "How much do you **charge**?" one hundred dollars per visit. " I'll **sleep on it**," said Jerry. Six months later the doctor met Jerry on the street. "Why didn't you ever come to see me again?" asked the psychiatrist. "For a hundred bucks a visit ? The bartender **cured** me for $10." "Is that so! How ? " "He told me to cut the legs off the bed! Ain't nobody under there now!!!"

心理医生

杰瑞去看心理医生。"医生，我有些不对劲。每次睡觉的时候，我都感觉有人在床下。我要疯了！""给我一年时间，"医生说，"每周来三次，我会治好你。""怎么收费呢？""每次一百美元。""我会认真考虑的。"杰瑞答道。六个月后医生和杰瑞在街上相遇了，"为什么你再也没来呢？"医生问。"一次一百块钱吗？有个酒吧服务生收了十块钱就把我治好了。""真的？他怎么做到的？""他让我把床腿锯掉。现在那儿没人了！"

★★★★★

Two robbers were robbing a hotel. The first robber said, "I hear **sirens**. Jump!"

The second one said, "But we're on the 13th floor!"

The first one **screamed** back, "This is no time to be **superstitious**!"

两个盗贼在一家旅馆偷东西。第一个说："我听到警报响了，快跳吧！"

第二个说："但是我们在 13 层啊！"

第一个朝他大喊道："都什么时候了，还这么迷信！"

★★★★★

A kid asked his dad, “Hey, Pop, can you write in the dark ? ”
The dad answered, “Sure. What do you want me to write ? ”
The boy said, “Your name on this **report card**.”

有个孩子问他爸爸：“嘿，爸，你能在黑暗中写字吗？”
爸爸回答：“当然。你要我写什么？”
男孩说：“在这个成绩单上写你的名字。”
★★★★★

A **tricky** girl said, “Mom, I got a one hundred in school today!” The mom replied, “Great, **sweetie**, tell me about it.” The girl **reluctantly** said, “Well, I got a twenty in math, a thirty in history and a fifty in spelling.”

一个狡猾的女孩说：“妈妈，我今天在学校得了一个 100 分！”
妈妈回答说：“太好了，小可爱。跟我说说情况。”
这个女孩不情愿地说：“嗯，我数学得了 20 分，历史得了 30 分，拼写得了 50 分。”

实战提升 Practising & Exercise

单词 & 词组

rob of 抢劫

shrink [ʃriŋk] *v.* 收缩；*n.* 精神病学家；心理学家

charge [tʃɑːdʒ] *n.* 收费

sleep on it 把问题留在第二天解决，考虑一下

cure [kjuə] *v.* 治愈，解决

siren ['saiərin] *n.* 汽笛，警报器；（救火车等）响着警报器行驶

scream [skriːm] *v.* 尖声喊叫

superstitious [ˌsjuːpə'stiʃəs] *adj.* 迷信的

report card 成绩单

tricky ['triki] *adj.* 狡猾的，机警的

sweetie ['swiːti] *n.* 恋人，爱人，糖果

reluctantly [r'lʌktəntli] *adv.* 不情愿地

知道不知道

13 在西方是个不吉祥的数字，希腊神话说，在哈弗拉宴会上共出席了 12 位天神。宴会当中，一位不速之客——烦恼与吵闹之神洛基忽然闯来了。这第 13 位来客的闯入，招致天神宠爱的快乐喜悦之神柏尔特送了性命。柏尔特死了，整个地球都陷入了黑暗和哀伤之中。从那一刻起，数字 13 便成了不祥之兆。

在圣经中也涉及到不吉利数字 13，背叛耶稣的传道者犹大是最后的晚餐中的第 13 个客人。因此在西方的大厦里通常没有 13 层楼或者 13 号的门牌。有一部著名的科幻电影叫《第十三层空间》(The Thirteenth Floor)，影片里的那套虚拟系统就在公司的第 13 层楼，也许编剧意在反讽连这套虚拟系统或许都是根本不存在的。

You can't call that food
你不能称那东西为食物

A father told his son, "When Lincoln was your age he walked ten miles to school every day." The kid replied, "Well, when he was your age, he was **president**!"

一个父亲告诉他的儿子："当林肯在你这个年纪的时候，他每天走10 里路去上学。"
孩子回答："嗯，当他在你这个年纪时，已经是总统了。"

★★★★★

A **cult** leader claimed that he **survived** on air. A doubter said, "I saw you eating French fries at McDonald's yesterday." The **guru** replied, "You can't call that food."

有一个教派的领导者宣称，他靠空气就能存活。
一个表示怀疑的人说："我昨天还看到你在麦当劳吃薯条。"
这位宗教领袖回答："你不能称那东西为食物。"

★★★★★

I knew a guy who played his radio only in the morning. When someone asked him why, he replied, "This is an **AM** radio."

我认识一个人，他只在早上收听广播。
当有人问他为什么时，他回答："（我的）这一台是 AM（调幅）收音机。"

★★★★★

The **Easter Bunny**, an honest lawyer, Santa Claus and a drunk find a fifty-dollar bill together. Can you guess who gets to keep it ? Of course, it's the drunk because the other three don't exist.

复活兔、诚实的律师、圣诞老人和一个醉汉同时看到一张 50 美元的钞票。你能猜到是谁会保留它吗?
当然是醉汉了，因为其他三个并不存在。

★★★★★

A boy told his mom she was **awful** at raising kids. She replied, "**Hold your tongue**. That's not true!" The boy said, "Then why do you send me to bed when I'm not tired and **wake me up** in the morning when I am ? "

一个男孩告诉他妈妈，说她在养育孩子方面做得很糟糕。
这位母亲回嘴说："住口，那不是真的！"
男孩说："那为什么你总是在我不困的时候叫我上床睡觉，在早上我困的时候叫醒我?"

实战提升 Practising & Exercise

单词 & 词组

president ['prezidənt] *n.* 总统，会长，校长，行长
cult [kʌlt] *n.* 宗派；崇拜
survive [sə'vaiv] *v.* 幸免于，幸存
guru ['guru:] *n.*（印度教）个人的宗教教师；（受下属崇敬的）领袖，头头
AM（amplitude modulation 的缩写）调幅，也是上午（ante meridiem）的缩写
Easter Bunny：复活节兔子。在欧洲的古老传说中，野兔是一种终日不闭眼的动物，它们能在黑夜里观看四周的动物。因此，野兔就代表着那黑夜中一轮皎洁的明月。再加上 Easter 日子是以春天月圆为基准，于是春天繁殖力很强的野兔就成为了 Easter 的一个象征。
awful ['ɔ:ful] *adj.* 可怕的，威严的，< 口 > 极度的，糟糕的
hold one's tongue 保持沉默，肃静
wake up 醒来

知道不知道

复活节是最古老最有意义的基督教节日之一。它庆祝的是基督的复活，即耶稣基督在十字架上受刑死后三天复活，象征着重生和希望。

复活节庆祝日期大致在 3 月 22 日至 4 月 25 日之间。典型的复活节礼物跟春天和再生有关系：鸡蛋、小鸡、小兔子、鲜花，特别是百合花是这一季节的象征。鸡蛋和小兔子在西方是新的生命和兴旺发达的象征。鸡蛋的本色象征太阳，把鸡蛋染成红色则象征生活幸福。

Who is nuts ?
谁是傻瓜？

Ten men **applied for** a job as an industrial spy. The interviewer gave each man a **sealed** envelope. They were ordered to deliver it to the fifth floor.

One man secretly **disobeyed** and opened his envelope. It read, "You're the right person for this job. Report to the **personnel department** immediately."

有 10 个男人去应征产业间谍的工作。面试者给每个人一个封好的信封。他们被命令把信封送到五楼。

有一个人偷偷地违反命令，打开了给他的信封。上面写着："你是这份工作最合适的人选。马上到人事部报到。"

★★★★★

At a wedding, a little boy asked his mother, "Mommy, why does the girl wear white ?" She answered, "The **bride** wears white because this is the happiest day of her life." The boy **thought about** this and said, "Why is the **groom** wearing black ? "

在一场婚礼上，一个小男孩问他的母亲："妈妈，为什么那女孩穿白衣服？"这位母亲回答道："新娘穿白衣服，是因为今天是她最快乐的一天。"这个男孩想了想然后说："那为什么新郎穿黑衣服？"

★★★★★

Do you know what Americans call a person in the White House who is **intelligent**, **honest** and **modest**？ The answer is "a tourist."

你知道美国人如何称呼白宫里聪明、诚实、谦虚的人吗？
答案是"观光客"。

★★★★★

Three gorillas fell out of a tree one by one. The first one was sick, the second was being a **copycat** and the third **gave in** to **peer** pressure.

有三只猩猩一个接一个地从树上掉下来。
第一只生病了，第二只盲目模仿，第三只屈服于同僚压力。

★★★★★

Who is **nuts**？

In a hospital for mentally disturbed people, when the doctor walked into the room of a patient, he saw him **dangling** from the ceiling. Being frightened, he called the nurse to come and pull him down for fear that the man might fall to his death. The nurse said: "Doctor, every day this patient thinks that he is a lamp, therefore, he often hangs from the ceiling!" The doctor said:

"No，you have to pull him down at once；otherwise，he'll die if he falls down."

After a pause，the nurse answered："But the light will **go out** after I pull him down!"

谁是傻子?

一家精神病院里，医生走进一个病人的房间，发现病人正吊在天花板上晃来晃去。医生吓坏了，担心病人摔下来一命呜呼，赶紧叫护士把病人拉下来。护士说："医生，这个病人每天都认为自己是一盏灯，所以常常把自己吊在天花板上。"医生说："不行，你还是得马上把他拉下来，免得他摔死。"

护士停顿了一下，说："可是，如果我把他拉下来，灯不就熄了吗?"

实战提升 Practising & Exercise

单词 & 词组

apply for 请求，申请

seal [siːl] *n.* 封铅，封条，印，图章，密封

disobey ['disə'bei] *v.* 违反，不服从

personnel department 人事部，人事科

bride [braid] *n.* 新娘

think about 考虑，回想

groom [gruːm] *n.* 马夫，新郎，男仆；喂马；修饰

intelligent [in'telidʒənt] *adj.* 聪明的，伶俐的，

honest ['ɔnist] *adj.* 诚实的，正直的

modest ['mɔdist] *adj.* 谦虚的，谦让的，适度的

copycat ['kɔpikæt] *n.* 无主见的家伙，复印机

give in 投降，屈服，让步，交上，宣布

peer [piə] *n.* 同等的人，贵族

nuts [nʌts] *adj.* 〈俚〉发疯的，傻的；坚果

dangling [dæŋglŋ] *n.* 悬挂的，悬浮的

go out 熄灭，停止运转

知道不知道

白色婚纱在维多利亚时代最为盛行。当年，维多利亚女王就是身穿漂亮的白色婚纱嫁给心上人的。从此，白色婚纱风靡全世界，一直到现在仍然是最受女孩们青睐的婚庆礼服，因为它象征着纯洁和忠贞。

Women's secrets
女人，不能说的秘密

◎ Women especially love a **bargain**. 女人特别喜欢便宜货。

◎ Women love to shop. It is the only area of the world where they feel like they're actually in control. 女人喜欢购物。她们觉得那是她们在这个世界上唯一能控制的领域。

◎ Women love to talk. Silence **intimidates** them and they feel a need to fill it，even if they have nothing to say. 女人喜欢交谈。沉默使她们不安，她们需要用交谈打破沉默，即使她们没什么可说的。

◎ Women need to feel like there are people worse off than they are. 女人需要感觉到别人不如她们。

◎ Women hate bugs. Even the **strong-willed** ones need a man around when there's a spider or a wasp involved. 女人讨厌虫子。当看到一只蜘蛛或黄蜂时，即使意志力很强的女人也需要一个男人在身旁。

◎ Women always go to public restrooms in groups. It gives them a chance to **gossip**. 女人经常结伴去公共卫生间。这是她们八卦的好机会。

◎ Women think all beer is the same. 女人觉得所有品牌的啤酒都是一个味儿。

◎ Women don't understand the appeal of sports. Men seek entertainment that allows them to escape reality. Women seek entertainment that reminds them of how horrible things could be. 女人不能领略体育节目的魅力。男人从那些能让他们逃离现实的东西中寻找娱乐，女人则从那些能提醒她们现实有多糟糕的东西中寻找娱乐。

◎ Women are paid less than men，except for one field：Modeling. 女人的薪水比男人低，只有一个行业例外——模特。

◎ Women do not know anything about cars，even if they drive a car themselves. 女人对汽车一无所知，即使她们自己开车。

◎ Women love to talk on the phone. A woman can visit her girl friend for two weeks，and upon returning home，she will call the same friend and they will talk for three hours. 女人喜欢煲电话粥。一个女人去看她的女朋友，她们一起生活了两个星期，她刚刚回家便会给这个女朋友打电话，然后会聊上 3 个小时。

◎ Women do not want an honest answer to the question，“How do I look？” 在“我看上去怎么样?”这个问题上，女人不想得到诚实的答案。

◎ "Oh, nothing," has an entirely different meaning in woman-language than it does in man-language. "哦，没什么。"这句话在女人的字典里的意思和在男人字典里的完全不同。

◎ All women will say that they are overweight, but don't agree with them about it. 所有女人都会说自己超重，但千万别对此表示赞同。

◎ Women can get out of speeding tickets by **pouting**. This will get men arrested. 面对超速行驶的罚单，噘嘴可以使女人免于处罚，却会使男人被拘留。

◎ Women don't really care about a sense of **humor** in a guy despite claims to the **contrary**. 女人并不真的在乎男人是否有幽默感，尽管她们声称幽默感很重要。

◎ Women will spend hours dressing up to go out, and then they'll go out and spend more time **checking out** other women. Men can never catch women checking out other men; women will always catch men checking out other women. 女人在出门前花费数小时化妆，然后她们出门，花更多时间注视其他女人。男人永远不会察觉女人注视着其他男人，而女人总能抓住男人注视着其他女人。

◎ The most **embarrassing** thing for women is to find another woman wearing the same dress at a formal party. 最让女人尴尬的就是在一个正式的聚会上，发现另一个女人穿着和自己同样的衣服。

实战提升 Practising & Exercise

单词 & 词组

bargain ['bɑːgin] *n.* 协定；便宜的东西
intimidate [in'timideit] *v.* 胁迫；威迫
strong-willed 意志坚强的，固执已见的
gossip ['gɔsip] *n.* 闲话，闲谈
pout [paut] *v.* 撅嘴，绷脸
humor ['hjuːmə] *n.* 幽默，心情，诙谐
contrary ['kɔntrəri] *adj.*（性质、方向或意义上）相反的
check out 付账后离开（旅馆）；查实；了解
embarrassed [im'bærəst] *adj.* 尴尬的，窘迫的

知道不知道

如何用英语骂女人

She is so neurotic and you can't imagine what she did to my cat. 她太神经质了，你想不到她对我的猫咪都干了些什么。

You are absolutely a disgrace of a human being. 你真是人类的耻辱。（其实这句话的听众不只女性，男人同样也没问题）

The bitch is back! 该死，又来了！（这句话也是 Elton John 与 Bernie Taupin 创作的一支非常著名的单曲。灵感来自 Taupin 的妻子，当时几个人正讨论 Caribou 专辑，但是突然间 Elton John 那传说中的爆脾气又来了，他大发无名火，惹得 Taupin 的老婆直呼"the bitch is back！"）

Are you a normal person ?
你精神正常吗？

The doctor lives downstairs

"Doctor," she said loudly, bouncing into the room, "I want you to say **frankly** what's wrong with me."

He **surveyed** her from head to foot. "Madam," he said at length, "I've just three things to tell you. First, your weight wants reducing by nearly fifty pounds. Second, your beauty could be improved if you used about one tenth as much **rouge** and **lipstick**. And third, I'm an artist, the doctor lives downstairs."

医生住在楼下

“医生”她冲进屋后大声说道。

“我想让你坦率地告诉我，我到底得了什么病。”

他从头到脚打量了她，然后大声说：“太太，我有三件事要对你说。第一，您的体重需要减少大约 50 磅；第二，如果您要用上十分之一的胭脂和口红，您的相貌将会变美。第三，我是一位画家——医生住在楼下。”

★★★★★

Are you a normal person ?

During a visit to the mental **asylum**, a visitor asked the director, "What is the **criterion** that defines a patient to be institutionalized ?" "Well..." said the director, "we fill up a bathtub, and we offer a teaspoon, a teacup, and a bucket to the patient and ask him to empty the bathtub." "Oh, I understand," said the visitor. "A normal person would choose the bucket as it is larger than the spoon or the teacup." "Noooooooo!" answered the director. "A normal person would pull the **plug**."

你精神正常吗?

一个参观者在参观一所精神病院的时候问院长,"你们是用什么标准来决定一个人是否应该进精神病院呢?""哦……"院长说,"是这样,我们先给一个浴缸放满水,然后我们给病人一个茶匙,一个茶杯和一个水桶去把浴缸里面的水放清。""哦,我明白了",参观者说,"正常人会选择水桶,因为水桶比茶匙和茶杯的容积大。""错了",院长回答道,"正常人会把浴缸塞子拔掉"。

★★★★★

Who's going deaf ?

A man tells a doctor, "I think my wife's going **deaf**. What can I do ?"

The doctor says, "Well, try to test her hearing. Stand some distance away from her and ask her a question. If she doesn't answer, move a little closer and ask again. Keep repeating this until she answers. That way we can see how bad the problem is."

The man goes home, sees his wife and says, "Hi honey, what's for dinner ?" He doesn't hear an answer, so he moves closer. "Honey, what's for dinner ?" He repeats this several

times, until he's standing right next to her.
Finally, she answers, "For the tenth time, I said we're having Pot Roast!"

谁要聋了?

丈夫告诉医生:"我想我的妻子快要聋了,我可以做些什么呢?"
医生告诉他:"嗯,先尝试测测她的听力吧。站在离她有一段距离的地方,问一个问题,如果她没有回答,走近一点再问一遍。一直重复直到她回答为止。这样我们就可以知道情况有多糟了。"
丈夫回到家,看见妻子便问:"亲爱的,晚餐吃什么?"他没有听到回答,于是走近一点再问:"亲爱的,晚餐吃什么呢?"这样重复了好几次,直到他就站在妻子旁边了。
终于,她回答了:"这是第十次了,我说我们吃炖肉!"

★★★★★

I think that I'm a chicken

Psychiatrist: What's your problem?
Patient: I think I'm a chicken.
Psychiatrist: How long has this been going on?
Patient: Ever since I was an egg!

我想我是一只鸡

精神病医师:你哪里不舒服?
病人:我认为我是一只鸡。
精神病医师:这种情况从什么时候开始的?
病人:从我还是一只蛋的时候开始。

实战提升
Practising & Exercise

单词 & 词组

frankly ['fræŋkli] *adv.* 坦白地，真诚地
survey [səː'vei] *n.* 测量，调查，俯瞰
rouge [ruːʒ] *n.* 口红，胭脂，
lipstick ['lipstik] *n.* 口红，唇膏
asylum [ə'sailəm] *n.* 庇护，救济院，精神病院
criterion [krai'tiəriən] *n.*（评判的）标准，尺度
plug [plʌg] *vt.* 堵，塞，插上，插栓
deaf [def] *adj.* 聋的

知道不知道

晒晒和 nut 有关的词汇和口语里常用到的句子吧：
nut 坚果，疯子，头，螺母
walnut 核桃
peanut 花生
chestnut 板栗
cashew 腰果
almond 杏仁
pistachio 开心果
hazelnut 榛子
nutcracker 胡桃夹子
a hard nut to crack 难以对付的人或者事
be nuts about 对……疯狂着迷
it costs peanuts. 很便宜。

Open one eye and close one eye
睁一只眼，闭一只眼

Wife：You see. **According to** the statistics on the paper，80% of those who have died of liver cancer have drunk alcohol.
Husband：It's okay. To my **investigation**，all these people eat meals.

妻子：你看这张报纸，据统计，死于肝癌的人 80% 都是喝酒的。
丈夫：那有什么？据我调查，死于肝癌的人 100% 都吃饭的。

★★★★★

One day，Eve asked Adam，“Do you really love me？”
Adam said helplessly，“Do I have any other choice？”

一天，夏娃问亚当：“你当真爱我吗？”
亚当无可奈何地回答：“我还有别的选择吗？”

★★★★★

A guy is reading his paper when his wife walks up behind him and **smacks** him on the back of the head with a frying pan. He asks, "What was that for ? " She says, "I found a piece of paper in your pocket with 'Betty Sue' written on it." He says, "Jeez, honey, 'Betty Sue' was the name of the horse I **bet on**." She shrugs and walks away.

Three days later he's reading his paper when she walks up behind him and smacks him on the back of the head again with the **frying pan**. He asks, "What was that for? "She answers, "Your horse **called**."

一个家伙正在看报纸，他的妻子走到他身后，用一只煎锅敲他的后脑勺。他问道："这是为什么？" 她说："我在你口袋里发现了一张写有'Betty Sue'的纸条。" 他说："哎呀，亲爱的，'Betty Sue'是我赌的那匹马的名字。" 她耸了耸肩，走了。

三天后，他正在看报纸，妻子走到他身后，又用一只煎锅敲他的后脑勺。他问："这又是为什么？" 她答道："你的马打电话来了。"

★★★★★

Wife talking to her husband (who reads the newspaper all day):

"I wish I were a newspaper so I would be in your hands all day. "

Husband: "I wish that too, so I could **change** you daily. "

妻子对整天坐在那里看报纸的丈夫说："我希望我就是报纸，这样你就可以整天把我捧在手上了。"

丈夫说："我也希望你是报纸，那样的话我可以天天换新的。"

★★★★★

A：What would you do if you find your husband **date** with another woman？

B：I'll open one eye and close one eye .

A：How kind you are!

B：No ，I 'll **shoot** him!

A：如果你发现你丈夫与别的女人约会你会怎么做?

B：我会睁一只眼，闭一只眼。

A：你太善良了！

B：不，我要射死他！

★★★★★

Why is he howling

Dentist：Please stop **howling**. I haven't even **touched** your tooth yet.

Patient：I know，but you are standing on my foot!

他为什么喊

牙医：请你不要再喊了！我还没碰你的牙呢。

病人：我知道，可是你正踩着我的脚呀！

实战提升
Practising & Exercise

单词 & 词组

according to 依照
Investigation [inˌvestiˈgeiʃən] *n.* 调查，研究
smack [smæk] *n.* 滋味，风味，拍击声
bet on 打赌
frying pan 煎锅，长柄平锅
call [kɔːl] *n.* 打电话，喊声，叫声，命令
change [tʃeindʒ] *n.* 改变，变化，找回的零钱，
date [deit] *n.* 日期，约会
shoot [ʃuːt] *n.* 射击，发射，摄影
howl [haul] *n.* 嚎叫，怒吼，嚎啕大哭
touch [tʌtʃ] *n.* 触觉，接触，触摸

知道不知道

上帝在东方造了一个伊甸园，并给里面配上了许多种活物。园中央有两棵树：生命树与智慧树。上帝造了亚当，让他去园中，告诉他说，除生命树和智慧树上的果子外，其他果子他都能吃。上帝派所有动物到亚当那里，亚当就给所有动物取了名。之后，上帝就让亚当好好睡一觉。亚当睡觉的时候，上帝取下他的一根肋骨，用这根骨头造了夏娃，这样，亚当就不会孤单了。亚当和夏娃光着身体，很幸福地生活在伊甸园里，与上帝和谐相处。

Happiness in dream
梦中的幸福

Camera

On our way to a wedding in Vermont，my husband and I realized we had forgotten our camera. We stopped at a general store and，hoping to purchase a cheap，**disposable** model. Sal asked the owner，“Do you have any of those throwaway cameras？”

“Look，fella，” replied the owner，“I don't care what you do with it after you buy it.”

照相机

在前往威蒙特参加一个婚礼的路上，我和丈夫意识到我们忘了带照相机。我们在一家百货商店门前停了下来，希望能够买到一种便宜的，一次性照相机。萨尔问店主：“你们有那种用了就扔的照相机吗？”

“我说，小伙子，”店主回答说，“我可不管你买了之后怎么处理它。”

★★★★★

To patch the hole of pants

A young man came home from work and found his bride upset. “I feel terrible，” she said. “I was pressing your suit and I burned a big hole in the seat of your trousers."

"Forget it," said her husband. "Remember that I've got an extra pair of pants for that suit."

"Yes," said the woman, cheering up. "And it's lucky you have. I used another pants to **patch** the hole."

补衣服

一位年轻的丈夫下班回到家里，发现新娘心烦意乱。"我心里太难受了，"她说，"我在给你熨西装时把裤子的臀部烧了个大洞。"

"没事儿，"丈夫安慰她说，"你忘了我这套衣服有两条裤子。"

"是的，"妻子高兴地说，"幸亏你还有一条，我后来就用它来补了这个洞了。"

★★★★★

Millionaire

CEO: "My wife made a **millionaire** out of me."

Assistant: "What were you before?"

CEO: "a **multimillionaire**."

百万富翁

CEO：我妻子使我成为百万富翁。

助手：以前你是什么?

CEO：千万富翁。

★★★★★

An **absent-minded** husband

I was accompanying my husband on a business trip. He carried his portable computer with him, and the guard at the airport gate asked him to open the case. It was locked, and the man waited patiently as my embarrassed **spouse** struggled to remember the **combination**. At last he succeeded.

"Why are you so nervous ? " I asked him.

"The numbers are the date of our **anniversary**." my husband **confessed**.

心不在焉的丈夫

我陪丈夫一起出差，他带着他的笔记本电脑。到了机场出口处时，有位检查员要他打开包。但是包锁上了，机场工作人员耐心地等着我那窘迫的丈夫设法回想起暗锁的密码。最后他终于想起来了。

"你为什么那么紧张呢? " 我问他。

"密码是我们的结婚纪念日。" 他承认道。

★★★★★

Happiness in dream

There was a wife who told her husband, "Last night I dreamed you bought me a **mink** coat and a **diamond ring**."

The husband put down his newspaper and said, "Fine! Tonight go back to sleep and wear them."

梦中的幸福

妻子告诉丈夫说："昨天晚上我梦见你给我买了一件裘皮大衣和一个钻戒。" 丈夫放下手中的报纸说："好啊！今晚再睡着时，你就穿戴上它们吧。"

实战提升
Practising & Exercise

单词 & 词组

disposable [dis'pəuzəbl] *adj.*（物品）一次性的；可有可无的
patch [pætʃ] *n.* 斑点，斑纹；修补
millionaire [ˌmiljə'nɛə] *n.* 百万富翁，大富豪
multimillionaire [mʌltimiljə'neə(r)] *n.* 亿万富翁
absent-minded [ˌæbsənt'maindid] *adj.* 心不在焉的，出神的
spouse [spauz] *n.* 配偶
combination [ˌkɔmbi'neiʃən] *n.* 结合，联合，合并，化合，化合物
anniversary [ˌæni'vəːsəri] *n.* 周年纪念
confess [kən'fes] *v.* 认错，供认
happiness ['hæpinis] *n.* 幸福
mink [miŋk] *n.* 貂皮
diamond ['daiəmənd] *n.* 钻石；方块（扑克牌的四种花色之一）
ring [riŋ] *n.* 戒指；环状物；铃声

知道不知道

不管是在梦里，还是真实生活里，偶尔做做 Day dream（白日梦）也不失为一种好的放松方式。不知大家有没有听过一位叫 Daydream 的钢琴师演奏的音乐，若是听到，一定会让你心动的。

Can pilots fly ?
飞行员会飞吗?

In the supermarket

The man approached a very beautiful woman in a supermarket and asked, "You know, I've lost my wife here in the supermarket. Can you talk to me for a couple of minutes ? "

"Why ? " she asks.

"Because every time I talk to a beautiful woman, my wife appears out of **nowhere**."

在超市里

在一个超市里，一个男子走向一位非常漂亮的小姐，对她说："我和我的妻子走散了，你能和我聊一会儿吗？"

"为什么呢？" 这个小姐问。

"因为每当我与漂亮小姐聊天时，我的妻子就会不知从什么地方冒出来。"

★★★★★

Relative by marriage

A husband and wife drove for miles in silence after a terrible **argument** in which neither would **budge**.

The husband pointed to a mule in a **pasture**. "Relative of yours ? " he asked.
"Yes," she replied. "By **marriage**."

婆家的亲戚

一对夫妻开着车出去，走了很长一段时间谁也不吭声。因为在这之前他们曾争吵得很厉害，并且谁也不肯让步。
丈夫指着牧场上的一头骡子问道："你亲戚吧？"
"没错，"她回答道，"婆家的亲戚。"

★★★★★

Won't be in at all

One morning a **colleague** said, "I need to leave early tomorrow." That afternoon he followed up with, "Looks like I'll be coming in late tomorrow, but if my coming in late runs into my leaving early, then I won't be in at all."

干脆不来了

一天上午，一个同事说："明天我要早一点走。"当天下午他又补充说："看来我明天要晚一点来。但是，如果我要来得晚，又得早走的话，那我明天干脆不来了。"

★★★★★

It's not that noticeable

There's a scar on my face from a car accident. A customer came into the **gas station** where I work, glanced at me and exclaimed, "My God, what happened to you ? " I told him and hoped that would be the end of it. But he kept pressing me for more information. Finally, he made his purchase and, just before walking away, said, "Hey, don't worry about it. It's not that **noticeable**."

那伤疤不是很明显

我脸上有一道车祸留下的伤疤。一位顾客走进我工作的加油站，看了我一眼就大呼小叫起来："我的天哪，你出什么事啦？"我告诉了他，希望就此打住。但是他继续追问更多的问题。最后，他买完东西要离开的时候说："嘿，别太在意。那伤疤不是很明显。"

★★★★★

Can pilots fly?

The Great Lakes Laboratory **employed** a licensed boat captain for its research **vessel**. It was common knowledge that the captain couldn't swim. When newcomers learned of this, they would often **approach** him about it, "Is it true? You, a boat captain, can't swim?" "No, I can't!" he replied. "Can **pilots** fly?"

飞行员会飞吗？

五大湖实验室雇用一位有执照的船长驾驶研究用的船。大家都知道这个船长不会游泳。当新来的人知道这事以后，他们常常会去问他："这是真的吗？身为船长你不会游泳？"他回答说："对，我不会！飞行员会飞吗？"

实战提升
Practising & Exercise

单词 & 词组

nowhere ['nəuhwɛə] *adv.* 不在任何地方；任何地方都不

argument ['ɑːgjumənt] *n.* 争执；理由

budge [bʌdʒ] *v.*（使）改变主意；让步

pasture ['pɑːstʃə] *n.* 牧场；牧草；放牧

marriage ['mæridʒ] *n.* 婚姻；（喻）结合

colleague ['kɔliːg] *n.* 同事，同行

gas station 加油站

noticeable ['nəutisəbl] *adj.* 明显的，值得注意的

employ [im'plɔi] *n.* 雇用，工作，职业

vessel ['vesl] *n.* 船，舰，容器

approach [ə'prəutʃ] *n.* 接近，交涉，通路，途径

pilot ['pailət] *n.* 飞行员，驾驶，带领

知道不知道

五大湖（Great Lakes）是位于加拿大与美国交界处的 5 座大型淡水湖泊，按面积从大到小分别为：苏必利尔湖（Lake Superior）、休伦湖（Lake Huron）、密歇根湖（Lake Michigan）、伊利湖（Lake Erie）和安大略湖（Lake Ontario）。除密歇根湖全属于美国之外，其他四湖为加拿大和美国共有。

这五个湖泊所组成的五大湖是世界上最大的淡水水域，总面积达 245，660 平方公里，有北美洲地中海之称。

Hi Dan!
你好，丹！

The traffic light's red

My wife needed **encouragement** to keep pedaling the exercise bike in gym. I said, "Close your eyes and imagine you're riding along Broadway in New York City. It will be more interesting." Inspired, she **cycled** on, but after a minute she stopped. "What's wrong?" I asked. "The traffic light's red," she replied.

红灯了

我太太需要一些鼓励才能继续蹬健身自行车。我说："你闭上眼睛，想象你是沿着纽约的百老汇大街在骑车。这样比较有趣。"在这一灵感的激发下，她继续蹬下去，但是仅仅一分钟她又停下了。我问她："怎么啦?"她回答说："红灯了。"

★★★★★

Honey, so do I!

We were discussing the "don'ts" of public speaking in the PR class I teach. "Don'ts" include a man reaching into his pant pocket and jangling change as he speaks, which is very **distracting**. To **illustrate** my point, I asked for a student volunteer, saying, "I need a man with coins in his pocket." What I got was a girl **yelling** out, "Honey, so do I!"

亲爱的，我也要！

在我教的公共关系课上，我们正在讨论公共场合讲话时“不要做什么”。其中有一项就是男人在讲话的时候，不要把手伸进裤子口袋，把硬币弄得哗哗响。这么做会分散注意力。为了阐明我的观点，我要一个学生做示范。我说：“我需要一个男人，口袋里有硬币。”结果，一个女孩大叫道：“亲爱的，我也要！”

★★★★★

Hi Dan!

A lawyer was reading out the **will** of a rich man: "To you, my loving wife Rose, who stood by me in **rough** times, as well as good, I leave her the house and $2 million." The lawyer continued, "To my daughter Jessica, who looked after me in sickness and kept the business going, I leave her the **yacht**, the business and $1 million." The lawyer concluded, "And, to my cousin Dan, who hated me, argued with me, and thought that I would never **mention** him in my will—well you are wrong. Hi Dan!"

你好，丹！

一位律师正在宣读一个富人的遗嘱：“我亲爱的太太罗丝，不论是顺境还是逆境，你都在我的身边。我给你留下房子和200万美元。我的女儿杰西卡，她在我生病的时候照顾我，维持生意继续运转。我把帆船、生意和100万美元留给她。我的表弟丹，你恨我，和我争吵，并且以为我在遗嘱里不会提到你的名字。你错了——你好，丹！”

★★★★★

A personal question

At the **cashier** one busy day the line grew quite long. There was much **grumbling** among those waiting, but one man **made light of** the situation. He approached a woman who was obviously very pregnant and tapped her on the shoulder. "Would you mind my asking a **persona**l question ? " he said. "Were you pregnant when you got in this line ? "

一个私人问题

在一个繁忙的日子，收银员那里排了很长的队。排队等待的人开始发牢骚，只有一名男子显得比较轻松。他走到一个显然已经怀孕很久的女人背后，拍拍她的肩膀说："我能不能问你一个私人问题，在你开始排队的时候有没有怀孕? "

实战提升
Practising & Exercise

单词 & 词组

encouragement [in'kʌrɪdʒmənt] *n.* 鼓励，支持（的事物）
cycle ['saikl] *n.* 循环；骑自行（摩托）车
distract [dis'trækt] *v.* 使分心，分散注意力
illustrate ['iləstreit] *vt.* 给……加插图；说明
yell [jel] *n.* 叫喊，叫着说
will [wil] *n.* 意图，决心；遗嘱
rough [rʌf] *adj.* 艰难的，粗糙的，粗鲁的，（味道、声音等）令人不快的
yacht [jɔt] *n.* 游艇，帆船
mention ['menʃən] *n.* 提及，说起
cashier [kæ'ʃiə] *n.* 收银员，出纳员
grumble ['grʌmbl] *vi.* 抱怨，牢骚
make light of 对……不在乎，轻视
personal ['pə:sənl] *adj.* 个人的，亲自的

知道不知道

公共场合讲话时“不要做什么”

做 public speaking 时，还有几个不要，譬如不要把手伸进口袋里（stick your hands in your pockets），不要手卡在腰带上（hook your thumbs under your belt），因为上述动作都会分散观众的注意力。

Half glass of water
半杯水

A man and his son were riding in the car. The man said to his son，“Could you check and see if the **direction lights** are working on your side of the car ？” His son looked out the window and said，“Yes，no，yes，no，yes，no，yes，no...”

有一个男人和他的儿子坐在车上。这个男人对他儿子说：“你能检查一下你那边的方向灯有没有坏吗？”儿子把头伸出窗外说：“有，没有，有，没有，有，没有……”

★★★★★

Half glass of water

To the **optimist**，the glass is half full. To the **pessimist**，the glass is half empty. To the engineer，the glass is twice as big as it needs to be.

半杯水

对于乐观主义者，这玻璃杯有一半是满的；对于悲观主义者，这玻璃杯有一半是空的。对于工程师，这玻璃杯比实际需要大了一倍。

★★★★★

Oh，Ohio

I **brag about** my home state of Ohio whenever I have a chance. One day，I told a friend，"You know，the first man in powered flight was from Ohio. The first man to orbit the earth was from Ohio. And the first man on the moon was from Ohio. " "Sounds like a lot of people are trying to get out of Ohio，" he **observed**.

哦，俄亥俄

只要一有机会，我就会吹嘘我的故乡俄亥俄。有一天，我对一个朋友说："你瞧，第一个用动力飞行的人是俄亥俄人；第一个绕地球轨道飞行的人也是俄亥俄人；第一个登上月球的人还是俄亥俄人。"他的评论是："看来好多人都想离开俄亥俄。"

★★★★★

Can I borrow your daughter？

A woman took her five-year-old daughter shopping with her. The little girl watched her mother try on **outfit** after outfit，exclaiming each time，"Mommy，you look beautiful ！" A woman in the next dressing room called out，"Can I borrow your daughter for a moment？"

我能不能借借你的女儿？

一位女士带着她五岁的女儿去购物。小姑娘看着她妈妈一件又一件地试穿衣服，每一次都惊叫道："妈妈，你真好看！"在隔壁更衣室的女人喊了起来："我能不能借你的女儿用一会儿？"

★★★★★

The meat department

My office is in a building **remodeled** from a former supermarket.

One day I overheard the receptionist giving directions over the phone. "Remember the old **grocery** store ? " she asked the caller. "You'll find us in the meat **department**."

肉食部

我的办公室设在由超市改装过的一座大厦里。有一天，我听见前台秘书在电话里描述我们的位置。她说："记得老杂货店吗？你能在肉食部找到我们。"

实战提升
Practising & Exercise

单词 & 词组

direction light 向灯
optimist ['ɔptimist] *n.* 乐观主义者
pessimist ['pesɪmist] *n.* 悲观主义者
brag about 对…自夸；吹嘘…
observe [əb'zə:v] *vt.* 观察；研究
outfit ['autfit] *n.* 全套装备，全套工具
remodel ['ri:'mɔdl] *vt.* 重建
grocery ['grəusəri] *n.* 杂货
department [di'pɑ:tmənt] *n.* 部，部门

知道不知道

汽车部件名词术语

引擎盖——bonnet ； hood
后备箱——boot ； trunk
挡泥板——mudflap
轮胎——tyre ； tire
后视镜（车内中央，矩形的）——rearview mirror
方向盘——steering wheel
安全带——seat belt
变速杆（排挡）——gear shift，shift lever
手刹车——hand-brake lever
脚刹车（踏板）——brake pedal
油门（踏板）——accelerator pedal
离合器（踏板）——clutch pedal

Make him a conductor
让他当指挥

To tune my cello

One of my friends, a **musician**, is always **upbeat**. Nothing gets her down. But when she developed ringing in one ear, I was concerned it might overwhelm even her. When I asked if her condition was especially annoying to a musician, she shook her head. "Not really," she said cheerfully. "The ringing sound is in the key of B flat, so I use it to tune my **cello** a half-tone lower."

给大提琴调音

我的一个音乐家朋友总是那么乐观，没有什么事能让她消沉。但是，当她的一只耳朵得了耳鸣之后，我担心这会让她受不了。我问她耳鸣是不是使音乐家特别恼火，她摇了摇头，高兴地说："这个耳鸣声正好是在降 B 调上，因此我用它把大提琴调低半个音。"

★★★★★

What was wrong ?

When I moved to California, I was a nervous wreck about earthquakes. My friend Lisa, who was born and raised there, was completely blase. I remember once when we pulled up to a light, her Honda began to shake. She looked worried until I **stammered**, "I think that we're having an earth quake. " "Thank goodness," Linda said. "I thought something was wrong with my car."

出什么问题了?

当我刚搬到加州住的时候，我对地震极为紧张。而我那位在加州土生土长的朋友丽莎却对此完全无动于衷。我记得有一次我们在等红灯的时候，她的本田车开始抖动起来。她看起来很担心，直到我结结巴巴地说："我想我们是碰到地震了。"她立刻松了一口气说道，"谢天谢地，我还以为是我的车出问题了。"

★★★★★

Make him a conductor

My musical director wasn't happy with the performance of one of our **percussionists**. Repeated attempts to get the drummer to improve failed. Finally, in front of the **orchestra**, the director said in **frustration**, "When a musician just can't handle his instrument, they take it away, give him two sticks and make him a drummer! " A whisper was heard from the percussion section: "And if he can't handle that, they take away one of his sticks and make him a **conductor**. "

让他当指挥

我们的乐队指挥对一位打击乐手的表现很不满意。他想让鼓手有所改进的多次努力都失败了。最后，指挥当着整个乐队的面生气地说："当一个音乐家不能玩好自己的乐器的时候，他们就把他的乐器拿走，给他两根棍，让他当鼓手。"这时候，从打击乐器那边传来耳语声："如果他还不能摆弄好它，就拿走一根棍，让他当指挥。"

★★★★★

I can turn him off

After earning my degree in broadcast journalism, I was fortunate to land a job as a **disc jockey** at a top-rated local radio station. One day before work, I stopped by my parents'house, where my mother was chatting with some friends. She introduced me to everyone and proudly mentioned that I had my own radio show. "How is it having a son who's a popular radio personality ? " asked one friend. "It's wonderful!" Mom replied with **glee**. "For the first time in his life, I can turn him off whenever I please."

我可以把他关掉

我在获得广播新闻学位以后，很幸运地在当地一家顶级广播电台里谋得一份流行音乐节目主持人的工作。有一天，我在上班之前到父母家里去了下。我妈正在和几个朋友聊天。她把我介绍给每一个人，并且骄傲地提到我已经有了自己的广播节目。有一个朋友问："有一个在电台工作的儿子感觉怎么样? " 妈妈高兴地说："太好了！这还是在他人生中头一回，只要我愿意，我就可以把他关掉。"

实战提升 Practising & Exercise

单词 & 词组

musician [mjuː'ziʃən] *n.* 音乐家
upbeat ['ʌpbiːt] *n.* 积极乐观的
cello ['tʃeləʊ] *n.* 大提琴
stammer ['stæmə] *n.* 结巴地说出，口吃
percussionist [pə'kʌʃənɪst] *n.* 打击乐器演奏者
orchestra ['ɔːkistrə] *n.* 管弦乐队
frustration [frʌs'treiʃən] *n.* 挫折，失败，沮丧
conductor [kən'dʌktə] *n.*（乐队）指挥，售票员，列车长，导体
disc jockey 电台的音乐节目主持人
glee [gliː] *n.* 高兴

知道不知道

Disk Jockey 简称 DJ。jockey 这个词是很早就有的，做名词是指专业的骑手；作动词是指挥马匹或让其他东西处于良好的运动状态。20 世纪 30 年代，广播进入了美国人的生活，信息传播的速度大大加快。1940 年，电视机又取代了广播，除新闻之外，大多数娱乐节目都转向电视播放。此时，广播希望通过某些方式夺回其在娱乐节目上的地位，于是新的意义上的 jockey 就出现了：数以万计的电台开始播放音乐录音带（discs），同时聘请熟悉音乐的人士担任解说。人们很喜欢这种娱乐方式，有些解说人因此而非常出名。逐渐地，电台播出的音乐录音带对听众选购录音带产生了很大影响，音乐制作人和唱片公司纷纷将录音带送到电台，希望多多宣传。于是，一个新的职产生了：disc jockeys 被用来指代那些音乐解说人，因为他们引导了听众的音乐欣赏口味和音乐本身的流行趋势。

A letter to her son
写给儿子的信

That's my son

It's every airplane passenger's **nightmare**—getting stuck near a crying baby. I was manning the ticket counter at a busy airport when the sound of a crying **infant** filled the air. As the next passenger stepped up to the desk, he glanced at the **tot** and rolled his eyes. "Don't worry," I said to him **cheerily**. "Chances are that baby won't be on your flight." Head shaking, he grimly replied, "Oh, I bet he will. That's my son."

那是我儿子

如果乘飞机的时候坐在啼哭的孩子附近，那简直就是一场噩梦。当我在一个繁忙的机场顶班帮助检票的时候，有一阵婴儿的哭闹声传过来。下一个乘客走到柜台跟前，看了一眼小家伙，把眼睛转过去。我安慰他说："别担心，很有可能这孩子不和你坐同一班飞机。"他摇摇头，无可奈何地说："他肯定要和我坐同一班飞机。他是我的儿子。"

★★★★★

A letter to her son

Dear Son,

I'm writing this slow because I know you can't read fast. We don't live where we did when you left. Your dad read in the paper that most accidents happen within twenty miles of home, so we moved. Won't be able to send you the address as the last family that lived here took the numbers with them for their new house, so they wouldn't have to change their address. Your sister had a baby this morning. I haven't found out whether it is a boy or a girl. So don't know if you are an Aunt or Uncle. It only rained twice this week, three days the first time and four days the second time. If you don't get this letter, please let me know and I will send another one.

Love, Mum

写给儿子的信

亲爱的儿子:

我在慢慢地给你写信，因为我知道你看信看不快。我们已经不住在你走的时候那个地方了。你爸爸看报纸上说大多数交通事故都发生在离家 20 英里的距离内，所以我们就搬家了。我现在不能告诉你我们的地址，因为原来住在这里的那家把门牌号拿到他们的新家去了，这样他们就不需要换地址了。今天早上你姐姐生了一个孩子。我还不知道是男孩还是女孩。所以也不知道你是当了阿姨还是舅舅。这个星期只下了两次雨，第一次下了三天，第二次下了四天。如果你收不到这封信，请你告诉我。我再给你写一封。

爱你的妈妈

★★★★★

Blind driver

The **stoplight** on the corner buzzes when it is safe to cross the street. I was crossing with a co-worker of mine, when she asked if I knew what the **buzzer** was for. I explained that it signals to blind people when the light is green. She responded, **appalled**, "What on earth are blind people doing driving ? "

盲人开车

当行人可以安全过马路的时候，马路拐角处的指示灯就会发出响声。我正和一位同事一起过马路，她问我知道不知道这响声是干什么用的。我说，这是给盲人的绿灯信号。她胆战心惊地问："盲人究竟为什么要开车?"

★★★★★

The opposite

If con is the opposite of pro, then congress is the opposite of progress ?

反义词

如果 con (反对) 是 pro (赞成) 的反义词，那么 congress (国会) 是 progress (进步) 的反义词吗?

实战提升 Practising & Exercise

单词 & 词组

nightmare ['naɪtmeə(r)] *n.* 噩梦，可怕的事情
infant ['infənt] *n.* 婴儿，幼儿
tot [tɔt] *n.* 幼儿；少量酒
cheerily ['tʃirili] *adv.* 快活地；兴高采烈地；爽快地
stoplight ['stɔpˌlait] *n.* 停止行进号志，红色尾灯，刹车灯
buzzer ['bʌzə] *n.* 有声信号，蜂音器
appall [ə'pɔːl] *vt.* 使惊骇，使充满恐惧

知道不知道

如何用英语问路和给别人指路

Excuse me，which bus goes to Chaoyang Park？请问到朝阳公园该乘几路车?
Bus No. 406. 406 路就行。
I'm afraid there is no direct bus. 恐怕没有直达车。
What stop is next？下一站是哪里?
Where do I get off for the museum？到博物馆要在哪儿下车?
Get off on Wang fujing Street. 在王府井大街下车就行。
Walk along the street and turn right at the corner. 沿着这条街直走，到了路口右拐。

He looks just like you
他长得真像你

You can have mine

A lady **inserted** an ‘ad’ in the **classifieds**：“Husband wanted”.
Next day she received a hundred letters.
They all said the same thing：“You can have mine.”

把我丈夫让给你

一位女士在分类广告栏目刊登了一则启事：“找丈夫”。
次日她收到了上百封信。
内容均是：“可以把我的丈夫让给你。”

★★★★★

He looks just like you

We brought our newborn son to the **pediatrician** for his first **checkup**. As he finished, the doctor told us, “You have a cute baby.” Smiling, I said, “I bet you say that to all new parents.” “No,” he replied, “just to those whose babies really are good-looking.” “So what do you say to the others？” I asked. “He looks just like you.”

他长得真像你

我们带着刚出生的儿子到儿科医生那里去做第一次健康检查。做完检查之后医生对我们说：“你们的孩子很好看。”我笑着说：“我想你对所有刚做爸爸妈妈的人都这么说。”他回答说：“不，我只是对长得真的好看的孩子的父母才这么讲。”我问：“那你对其他人怎么说呢？”“他长的真像你。”

★★★★★

This is Lisa. Can I help you ?

As customer-service reps, we hear a beep telling us a custome's on the line, and we're on. We repeat the same phrases so often that we can do the job in our sleep. One day a co-worker had heart surgery. In her **anesthetized stupor** following her operation, she heard the beep of the heart monitor and groggily said, "This is Lisa. Can I help you ? "

我是丽莎，能为您做什么?

作为顾客服务代表，当我们听到“嘀”的一声就知道有一个顾客在电话线上，我们就上线。我们反反复复讲那几句同样的话，以至睡着了也能讲。有一天，一个同事做心脏手术。在手术之后，她仍然处于麻药的昏睡之中。听到心电监护仪发出的“嘀嘀”声，她虚弱地说：“我是丽莎，能为您做什么？”

★★★★★

Only when he's DRUNK

A man is driving with his wife, when he is **pulled over** by a policeman. "Sir," says the cop. "You , were going 60 in a 50." "No, I wasn't. "Yes, you were," says the wife. "Keep quiet!" says the man, angrily. "And you were't wearing a **seat belt**," says the cop. "Yes, I was." "No, you weren't," says the wife. "SHUT UP!" says the man, really angry. "Ma'am," asks the cop, "is he always rude and violent ?" "Only when he's DRUNK."

他只是在喝醉的时候才这样

有个男人开着车，车里坐着他老婆。一位警察让他停在路边，对他说："先生，你在限速 50 的路上开 60。""我没有。"他老婆说："你是开那么快。"男人生气地说："闭嘴！"警察说："你还没有系安全带。""我系了。"他老婆说："你是没有系。"男人非常生气地说："闭嘴！"警察问："夫人，他一直是那么粗鲁和野蛮吗？""他只是在喝醉的时候才这样。"

实战提升
Practising & Exercise

单词 & 词组

Insert [in'sə:t] *n.* 插入，刊登
classified ['klæsifaid] *v.*（报纸、杂志的广告或广告版）分类的
pediatrician [ˌpi:diə'triʃən] *n.* 小儿科医师
checkup ['tʃekʌp] *n.* 检查，核对，体格检查
anesthetized ['ənesθiˌtaizd] *v.* 使麻醉，使麻木
stupor ['stju:pə] *n.* 恍惚，昏迷，惊愕
pull over 靠向路边
seat belt 座椅安全带

知道不知道

如何用英文打电话和接电话

Who do you want to speak with (talk to)? 请问找哪位?
Nina，please. 尼娜。
Hold on，please. 请等一下。
Oh，She is in the office of General Manager. Any message ? 哦，她现在总经理办公室。要留言吗?
No. I'll call later. 不必了，我晚点再打来。

That record will stand forever
这个纪录永远不会被打破了

You didn't have that problem

"Your grandmother and I are going out to dinner," I said to my teenage daughter, Lisa. "Do you want to join us?" "No way," she answered grumpily. "I'm going to stay home and study." That evening my mother asked if Lisa was feeling well. "She's okay," I said, "just a little **cranky**." "Intelligent children can be very **temperamental**," my mother sighed. "I am lucky that you didn't have that problem."

你没有那样的问题

我对十几岁的女儿丽莎说："我和你姥姥一起出去吃晚饭，你要不要和我们一起去？"她烦躁地回答："我才不去呢。我要在家里学习。"那天晚上我妈问我丽莎是不是生病了。我说："没有。她只是脾气有点坏。"我妈叹了一口气说："聪明的孩子会喜怒无常。我很幸运，你没有那样的问题。"

★★★★★

That record will stand forever

Back at my high school for the tenth reunion, I met my old **coach**. Walking through the **gym**, we came upon a **plaque** on which I was still listed as the record holder for the longest **softball** throw. Noticing my surprise, the coach said, "That record will stand forever." I was about to make some modest **disclaimer** that records exist to be broken, when he added, "We stopped holding that event years ago."

这个纪录永远不会被打破了

高中毕业十年以后，我回母校团聚，碰到以前的教练。我们穿过体育馆的时候，看到一块牌匾，上面刻着我的名字，我仍然是垒球投掷最远纪录保持者。注意到我的诧异，老教练说："这个纪录永远不会被打破了。"当我刚想谦虚几句说纪录的存在就是为了被打破时，他补充说："我们几年前就取消这项比赛了。"

★★★★★

Pushed the wrong button

Flying through the Midwest in the summertime means one thing: **turbulence**. Just after a teenager girl had entered the bathroom, we hit a patch of very rough air. After the **bumps** had **subsided**, she exited the bathroom, a look of sheer terror etched on her face. "Are you all right ?" 1 asked. "That turbulence was so bad." "So that's what it was," she said. "I thought I'd pushed the wrong button."

按错了按钮

夏季在美国中西部飞行就意味着一件事：涡流。一个十几岁的女孩刚进入厕所，我们的飞机就碰到一片非常不稳定的气流。等颠簸平息下来以后，她从厕所里出来了，一脸恐惧的模样。我问她："你没事吧？这股涡流可够厉害的。"她说："原来是这么一回事。我还以为是因为我按错了按钮呢。"

★★★★★

The oldest thing in my house

My 12-year-old daughter asked me, "Mom, do you have a baby picture of yourself? I need it for a school project." I gave her one without thinking to ask what the project was. A few days later I was in her classroom for a **parent-teacher** meeting when I noticed my face pinned to a mural the students had created. The title of their project was "The oldest thing in my house."

我家里最老的东西

我 12 岁的女儿问我："妈妈，你有小时候的照片吗？我要用来做学校的作业。"我也没问她是什么作业，就给了她一张。过了几天，我到她教室去参加家长会，发现我的脸被钉在学生们弄的一张壁画上。而她们作业的名字叫"我家里最老的东西"。

实战提升
Practising & Exercise

单词 & 词组

cranky ['kræŋki] *adj.* 古怪的
temperamental [ˌtempərə'mentl] *adj.* 易激动的，喜怒无常的
coach [kəutʃ] *n.* 教练，旅客车厢
gym [dʒim] *n.* 体育馆，健身房
plaque [plɑːk] *n.* 饰板，匾
softball ['sɔftbɔːl] *n.* 垒球
disclaimer [dis'kleimə(r)] *n.* 放弃；拒绝；不承诺
turbulence ['tɜːbjʊləns] *n.*（空气、水等的）紊流，湍流；动乱，骚乱，波动
bump [bʌmp] *v.* 碰撞，猛撞
subside [səb'said] *v.* 下降，下陷，减弱，平息下来
parent-teacher meeting 家长会

知道不知道

想想你家里最老的东西是什么呢？是一张旧照片，一枚铜钱，还是老家后院里的那棵柿子树？你知道吗，现在还活着的，最古老的树可能要属于长在美国的狐尾松（foxtail pine）了，它们有的已经有 4000 多岁了呢。它们生长在美国西部的干燥高山上，因为松果上的鳞片长得像狐尾而得此名。

Logic reasoning
逻辑推理

My mom puts me in the stroller too

While I sat in the reception area of my doctor's office, a woman rolled an elderly man in a **wheel chair** into the room. As she went to the receptionist's desk, the man sat there, alone and silent. Just as I was thinking I should make small talk with him, a little boy slipped off his mother's lap and walked over to the wheelchair. Placing his hand on the man's, he said, "I know how you feel. My mom makes me ride in the **stroller** too."

我妈妈也把我放在手推车里面

我在医生诊所的接待室等候的时候，一个女人推着坐在轮椅里的老人进来。在她去接待员那里时，老人孤零零地坐在那里，一声不响。我正想上去和他聊聊天，一个小男孩从他妈妈膝盖上滑下来，朝轮椅走去。他把手放在老人的手里，说："我了解你的感觉。我妈妈也把我放在手推车里面。"

★★★★★

A Pledge

Grandpa was celebrating his 100th birthday, and everyone was complimenting him on how well he looked.

"I'll tell you the secret," he said. "My wife and I were married seventy-five years ago. On our wedding night we **made a pledge** that whenever we had a fight, the one who proved wrong would go out and take a walk. I have been in the open air continuously for the past seventy-five years."

誓约

爷爷过一百岁生日，大家都祝贺他，说他看上去很健康。

"我来告诉你们这里面的秘密，"他说。"我和妻子结婚七十五年了。在新婚之夜我们订了一个誓约，那就是无论我们什么时候发生争吵，谁被证明错了，谁就到外面去散一圈步，我已经在外面一直待了七十五年了。"

★★★★★

A family quarrel

The young newly-weds quarreled.

At last she could bear it no longer and burst into tears.

"I don't want to have anything to do with you any more.

I'm **packing up** my things and going off to mother."

"Fine, my dear," said the husband.

"Here are the **traveling expenses**." She counted the money.

"What about the money for the return ticket?"

家庭的争吵

一对年轻的新婚夫妇吵架了。最后妻子终于忍不住哭了起来。

"我不想跟你有任何瓜葛了。我要去收拾东西，离开这里回娘家去。"

"好，亲爱的，"丈夫说，"我给你路费。"她数了数钱。"还有回来的路费呢。"

★★★★★

Logic reasoning

A fourth-grade teacher was giving her pupils a lesson on **logic**. "Here is the situation," she said. "a man is standing up in a boat in the middle of a river, fishing. He loses his balance, falls in, and begins **splashing** and yelling for help. His wife hears the **commotion**, knows that he can't swim, and runs down to the **bank**. Why do you think she ran to the bank?"

A girl raised her hand and asked, "to draw out all of his **savings**?"

逻辑推理

小学四年级的教师正在给学生们上一堂逻辑课。她举了这么一个例子："有这样一种情况，一个男人在河中心的船上钓鱼，突然失去重心掉进了水里。于是他开始挣扎并喊救命。他的妻子听到了喊声，知道他并不会游泳，于是就急忙跑向河岸。谁能告诉我这是为什么?"一个女生举手答道，"是不是去取他的存款?"

★★★★★

Eating out

When the bill arrives, Mark, Chris, Eric and Tom will each throw in a $20, even though it's only for $32.50. None of them will have anything smaller and none will actually admit they want change back. When the women get their bill, out come the pocket calculators.

外出就餐

买单的时候，阿麦，阿克、阿力和阿汤每人都甩出20块钱，虽然其实一共只吃了32块5。没人有更小的票子了，也没人愿意承认他们其实想把票子破开。女人买单时，每人掏出个计算器。

实战提升
Practising & Exercise

单词 & 词组

wheel chair 轮椅
stroller ['strəulə] *n.* 婴儿推车
make a pledge 许诺，发誓
pack up 打包，收拾
traveling expenses 差旅费
logic ['lɔdʒik] *n.* 逻辑，推理方法
splash [splæʃ] *n.* 拍水，戏水
commotion [kə'məuʃən] *n.* 混乱，喧闹，骚动
bank [bæŋk] *n.* 在英语中除了我们平时很熟悉的"银行"之外，还有"河岸"的意思。
savings ['seiviŋz] 储蓄

知道不知道

你一定没想到吧，其实现实生活中，大多数人每天说的话都有逻辑错误。逻辑有其自身的规律，不管使用什么概念和命题，进行何种推理和论证，都必须遵守最基本的逻辑规律。否则，人们的思维就会出现错误。常见的逻辑错误有偷换概念、偷换论题、自相矛盾、模棱两可、循环定义、同语反复、概念不当并列、因果倒置、循环论证、推不出等。当你和别人辩论时，可能总觉得说不过别人，其实并不一定是别人真的有理，而是他们采用了上述你没有觉察到的逻辑错误说话术，让你哑口无言，一时无法应答。比如：司马光夫人说："我要去看花灯。"司马光说："家中这么多灯，何必去看？"司马光夫人说："我要去看游人。"司马光说："家中这么多人，何必出去看？"犯的就是偷换概念的逻辑错误。

Men are from Mars，Women are from Venus
男人来自火星，女人来自金星

Money

A man will pay $2 for a $1 item he needs. A woman will pay $1 for a $2 item that she doesn't need，but it's on sale.

钱

用得着的东西，要是值 1 块钱却卖 2 块，男人也会买；用不着的东西，要是值 2 块钱但只卖 1 块，女人也会买。

★★★★★

Bathrooms

A man has five items in his bathroom：a toothbrush，**shaving cream**，**razor**，a bar of soap，and a **towel** from the Marriott. The average number of items in the typical woman's bathroom is 337. A man would not be able to **identify** most of these items.

浴室

男人浴室里五件宝：牙刷，刮胡膏，剃须刀，一块肥皂，一块毛巾。一般的女人浴室里平均有 337 样东西，其中的大多数，男人不知道那是干啥用的。

★★★★★

Arguments

A woman has the last word in any argument. Anything a man says after that... is the beginning of a new argument.

争论

任何争论都是由女人来说最后一句话。男人在此之后说的任何话……都是开始新的争吵。

★★★★★

Cats

Women love cats. Men say they love cats，but when women aren't looking，men **kick** cats.

猫

女人喜欢猫。男人说他们也喜欢，但当女人看不到时，男人踢猫。

★★★★★

Success

A successful man is one who makes more money than his wife can spend. A successful woman is one who can find such a man.

成功

成功的男人挣到的钱比他太太花的要更多；成功的女人就是能找得到这么个男人。

★★★★★

Marriage

A woman marries a man expecting he will change，but he

doesn't. A man marries a woman expecting that she won't change! And she does.

婚姻

女人嫁给一个男人，希望他能改变，可是他不会；男人娶了一个女人，希望她永远不变，可她变了。

★★★★★

Future

A woman worries about the **future** until she gets a husband. A man never worries about the future until he gets a wife.

未来

女人直到找到丈夫前都在担心未来；男人直到找到妻子前从不担心未来。

实战提升 Practising & Exercise

单词 & 词组

shaving cream 刮胡膏，剃须膏
razor ['reizə] *n.* 剃刀，刮面刀
towel ['tauəl] *n.* 毛巾，纸巾
identify [ai'dentifai] *n.* 辨认，识别
kick [kik] *n.* 踢
future ['fju:tʃə] *adj.* 将来的，未来的

知道不知道

《男人来自火星，女人来自金星》是美国著名心理学博士约翰·格雷写的一本畅销书。这本书是获得与异性完美关系的最佳指南，它对男人和女人达到完美沟通做出了巨大贡献。

当女人对婚姻和爱情感到沮丧和失望，最好提醒自己：男人来自火星，女人来自金星。这样你就不会以为，必是伴侣出现了问题，才使得你们产生冲突，感情不和。你也不会认定，感情本身不成熟，才是"罪魁祸首"。无视男女的差异，对于现实情况做出的评估，就极可能是错误的。认识到男人和女人的不同，你就能理顺思路，对问题重做解释和澄清，调整和反馈，让不利的局面得以改观，让心头的阴霾迅速消散。

Which woman？
哪一位女人？

Anxious

The wife says to the neighbor: “ My husband has not returned all the night；I do not know where he went . It really gives me a **hangup**!”

An **insider** says: “ **Let it be**. Would you know where he went，I dare to say that you would be more anxious .”

着急

妻子对邻居说：“丈夫一晚上都没回家，也不知道他干什么去了，真叫我着急！”

一个知情人说：“算了，你要知道他干什么去了，我敢说你会更着急。”

★★★★★

Honey，We've got a little car trouble

A wife said to her husband，“We've got trouble with the car；it has water in the **carburetor**.”

The husband **exclaimed**，“Water in the carburetor ? That's **ridiculous**!” The wife repeated，“I tell you，the car has water in the carburetor." The husband said, "But you don't even know what a carburetor is! Where's the car?" And the wife replied, "In the swimming pool!"

咱们的车出了点"小问题"

有位太太对先生说："我们的车子出问题了！化油器进水了。"先生说："化油器进水？真是荒谬！"太太重复道："我告诉你，车子的化油器进水了！"先生说："可是你连化油器是什么都搞不清楚啊！车子在哪儿？"太太回答："游泳池里！"

★★★★★

The same service

A man who had been married for ten years was consulting a marriage **counselor**.

"When I was first married, I was very happy. I'd come home from a hard day down at the shop, and my little dog would race around barking, and my wife would bring me my slippers. Now everything's changed. When I come home, my dog brings me my slippers, and my wife barks at me."

"I don't know what you're complaining about," said the counselor, "You're still getting the same service."

同样的服务

有位结婚十年的男人，正向婚姻顾问请教。

"新婚时我非常幸福。在市区的商店里累了一天，回到家里，小狗围着我又跑又叫，妻子忙给我拿来拖鞋。现在一切都变了。小狗给我叼来拖鞋，妻子对我又喊又叫。"

"我不知道你有什么可抱怨的，"顾问说，"你得到的服务还是同样的嘛。"

★★★★★

Which woman？

One evening I drove my husband's car to the shopping mall. On my return，I noticed how dusty the outside of his car was and cleaned it up a bit.When I finally entered the house，I called out. "The woman who loves you the most in the world just cleaned your **headlights** and **windshield**."

My husband looked up and said，"Mom's here？"

哪一位女人？

一天晚上我开着丈夫的车去购物，回来后发现车身沾满灰尘，于是擦洗了一阵。最后我走进屋里时大声喊道："世界上最爱你的女人刚擦洗了你的车灯和挡风玻璃。"

我丈夫抬头看了看，说："妈妈来了？"

实战提升 Practising & Exercise

单词 & 词组

hangup ['hæŋʌp] *n.* 焦虑
insider [in'saidə(r)] *n.* 知情人
let it be 随便……好了
carburetor [kɑ:bə'retə(r)] 汽化器，化油器
exclaim [iks'kleim] *v.*（由于强烈的情感或痛苦而）呼喊，惊叫，大声说
ridiculous [ri'dikjuləs] *adj.* 可笑的，荒谬的
counselor ['kaunsələ] *n.* 顾问，法律顾问
headlight ['hedlait] *n.* 汽车前灯
windshield ['windʃi:ld] *n.* 挡风玻璃，防风罩

知道不知道

《Let it be》是一张名义上 Beatles 合作的最后一张唱片，本来这张唱片应该叫做《Get back》，是因为 Pual 并不想乐队就此解散而做的最后努力，可是计划还是不幸的流产了,《Get back》也就被《Let it be》代替了。

When I find myself in times of trouble，
Mother Mary comes to me
Speaking words of wisdom，
let it be
And in my hour of darkness
she is standing right in front of me
Speaking words of wisdom，let it be
Let it be，let it be，let it be，let it be...

Get the kid
让小的干吧

Get the kid

A bit of advice for those about to retire. If you are only 65，never move to a **retirement** community. Everybody else is in their 70s，80s，or 90s. So when something has to be moved，lifted or loaded，they yell，“Get the kid.”

让小的干吧

这里想对将要退休的人提一点忠告。如果你只有 65 岁的话，千万别进退休社区。因为那里的人都七八十岁或者八九十岁了。每当要搬东西，抬东西或者装东西时，他们会喊，“让小的干吧。”

★★★★★

Are you using your **mower** this afternoon？

Mr. Johnson：Are you using your mower this afternoon？

Mr. Smith：Yes.

Mr. Johnson：Fine. Then can I borrow your tennis racket，since you won't be needing it？

约翰逊先生：今天下午你准备用割草机吗?

史密斯先生：是的。

约翰逊先生：太好了。既然您不用网球拍，那我可以借用一下吗？

★★★★★

Class and Ass

Professor Laurie of Glasgow put his notice on his door: “Professor Laurie will not meet his classes today.”

A student，after reading the notice，rubbed out the “c”.

Later Professor Laurie came along，and entering into the spirit of the joke，rubbed out the “l”.

班和笨驴

格拉斯哥的劳里教授在门上贴了这样一个通知：“劳里教授今天的课程取消。”

一个学生读了通知后，擦掉了字母“c”（lass：姑娘）。

后来劳里教授来了，也想开开玩笑，他擦掉了字母“l”（ass：笨驴）。

★★★★★

A little girl was lost，so she went up to a policeman and said，“I've lost my mom!” The cop said，“What's she like？” The little girl replied，“Shopping and **gossiping**!”

有一个小女孩走丢了，于是她走到一个警察跟前说：“我妈妈不见了！”

这个警察说：“她什么样子？”

小女孩回答：“买东西和说闲话！”

★★★★★

Contented married life

A man was telling one of his friends the secret of his **contented** married life, "My wife makes all the small decisions," he explained, "and I make all the big ones, so we never **interfere** in each other's business and never get annoyed with each other. We have no complaints and no arguments."

"That sounds reasonable," answered his friend sympathetically. "And what sort of decisions does your wife make?"

"Well," answered the man, "she decides what jobs I **apply for**, what sort of house we live in, what **furniture** we have, where we go for our holidays, and things like that."

His friend was surprised. "Oh?" he said. "And what do you consider important decisions then?"

"Well," answered the man, "I decide who should be Prime Minister, whether we should increase our help to poor countries, what we should do about the **atom bomb**, and things like that."

令人满意的婚姻生活

一个男人告诉他的朋友自己婚姻幸福美满的秘密。"小事都由我妻子决定，"他解释说："而我只管大事，我们从不互相干涉，从不生对方的气。我们从来没有抱怨、没有争吵。"

"听起来很有道理，"他的朋友深有同感，"哪些事情是由你妻子作决定呢？"

"嗯，"那个人回答说："她决定我申请什么工作，我们住什么房子，买什么家具，去哪里度假这些事情。"

他的朋友很惊奇地问道："哦？那么你决定哪些重要事情？"

"嗯，"他回答："我决定谁来当首相，我们是否要增加对贫困国家的援助，怎么处理原子弹等等这些问题。"

★★★★★

All the cigarettes will be on fire sooner or later

Mary was so disgusted at her husband's cigarette smoking that she complained to him one day.

'I hope that all the cigarette factories will catch fire someday.'

'Don't worry, dear. All the cigarettes will be on fire sooner or later.' He said with a smile.

所有的烟卷都会点着的

玛丽非常讨厌丈夫吸烟，一天她对丈夫抱怨说："我希望有一天所有卷烟厂都失火。"

"不用担心，亲爱的，所有的烟卷迟早都会点着的。"他笑着说。

★★★★★

A man goes to church and starts talking to God.

He says: "God, what is a million dollars to you ?" and God says: "A penny", then the man says: "God, what is a million years to you ?" and God says: "a second", then the man says: "God, can I have a penny ?" and God says: "In a second."

一男子进入教堂和上帝对话。

他问："主啊，一百万美元对你意味着多少？"上帝回答："一便士。"男子又问："那一百万年呢？"上帝说："一秒钟。"最后男子请求道："上帝，我能得到一便士吗？"上帝回答："过一秒钟。"

实战提升 Practising & Exercise

单词 & 词组

retirement [ri'taiəmənt] *n.* 退职，退休
mower ['məuə] *n.* 割草机
fake [feik] *n.* 假货，欺骗
gossip ['gɔsip] *n.* 闲话，闲谈
contented [kən'tentid] *adj.* 满足的，心安的
interfere [ˌintə'fiə] *vi.* 干涉，干预
apply for 请求，申请
furniture ['fəːnitʃə] *n.* 家具，设备
atom bomb 原子弹

知道不知道

都说全世界属中国人的思维最复杂，说话曲里拐弯的，没想到老外也有这样的。据说中国人重直觉（intuition），英美人重实证（evidence），中国人重形象思维（figurative thinking），英美人重逻辑思维（logical thinking）。

I don't want Him to know I'm here.
我不想让主知道我在这里

I don't want Him to know I'm here.

A **distinguished** clergyman and the elders from his congregation attended an out-of-town meeting that did not finish until rather late. They decided to have something to eat before going home, but unfortunately the only spot open was a **seedy** bar-and-grill with a questionable **reputation**.

After being served, one of the elders asked the **clergyman** to say grace. 'I'd rather not', the clergyman said, 'I don't want Him to know I'm here.'

我不想让主知道我在这里

一位著名牧师和他教区的几位老人出席城外会议，他们直到天黑才开完会。于是打算在回家前吃点东西。但很不巧只有一家名声不好的下等酒吧烤菜馆开着门。

饭后，一位老人要牧师祈祷。“我想我是免了，”牧师说。“我不想让主知道我在这里。”

★★★★★

Tom：William has asked me for a loan of five pounds. Should I be doing right in lending it to him？

Jack：Certainly.

Tom：And why？

Jack：Because otherwise he would try to borrow it from me.

汤姆：威廉向我借五英镑。我该不该借给他?

杰克：当然应该了。

汤姆：为什么?

杰克：否则他就该跟我借了。

★★★★★

An adult decision

The year before my son turned 18，he **constantly** pleaded to be allowed to a have **tattoo**，but I refused to sign **permission** for one. He argued that soon he would be a man and he should be able to make adult decisions. Sure enough，a few days after his 18th birthday，he come home with a tattoo. Although I was not happy about this，I was curious to see what symbol of **masculinity** he had chosen. There，on his shoulder，was a two-inch **image** of **Mickey Mouse**.

成年人的抉择

我儿子十八岁前的那一年，常常向我提出准许他文身。但我拒绝允许他这么做。他争辩说他不久就要成为男子汉了，并说他应该能够做出成年人的抉择了。果然，十八岁生日的几天后，他文了身，回到家里。尽管我对此感到不高兴，但出于好奇，我想看看他选择了什么雄性象征物。原来他在肩上文了一个两英寸长的米老鼠像。

★★★★★

HI lady!

If you kiss her，you are not a gentleman

If you don't，you are not a man

If you praise her，she thinks you are lying

If you don't，you are good for nothing

If you agree to all her likes，she is abusing

If you don't，you are not understanding

If you make romance，you are an ‘experienced man’

If you don't you are half a man

If you visit her too often，she thinks it is boring

If you don't，she accuses you of double crossing

If you are well dressed，she says you are a playboy

If you don't，you are a dull boy

If you are jealous，she says it's bad

If you don't ，she thinks you do not love her

If you attempt a romance，she says you didn't respect her

If you don't，she thinks you do not like her

If you are a minute late，she complains it's hard to wait

If she is late，she says that's a girl's way

嗨，女人！

吻她吧，不够君子

不吻吧，不象汉子

夸她吧，说你欺骗

不夸吧，说你笨蛋

顺她吧，说你气管炎

不顺吧，不善解人意

太浪漫，疑你老练

太规矩，魅力不足

常看她，招她厌烦

少去点，怨你猎艳

穿得好，说你花心

邋遢些，缺个心眼

吃醋吧，你太狭隘

大度点，说你不爱

求欢吧，不够尊重

安分吧，不够爱宠

你晚了，她等得烦

她晚了，女孩特权

实战提升 Practising & Exercise

单词 & 词组

distinguished [dis'tiŋgwiʃt] *adj.* 卓著的，高贵的
reputation [ˌrepju(:)'teiʃən] *n.* 名誉，名声
clergyman ['klə:dʒimən] *n.* 牧师，教士
Seedy ['si:di] *adj.* 多种子的，服饰破旧的
constantly ['kɔnstəntli] *adv.* 不断地
tattoo [tə'tu:] *n.* 纹身
permission [pə(:)'miʃən] *n.* 允许
masculinity [ˌmæskju'liniti] *n.* 阳性，男性
image ['imidʒ] *n.* 形象，肖像
Mickey Mouse 米老鼠

知道不知道

pastor 是新教（Protestant Christianity）中对牧师的称呼，可以用做头衔，后面可以跟姓，也可以跟名。
minister 牧师，基督教工作者。这个词不能用来做称呼，只是描述身份。
reverent 牧师，但这是一个抬头，称呼。reverent 在称呼上更显得正规，pastor 显得亲切、随意。
priest 牧师，祭司。天主教的神职人员一般叫 priest。使用此词时，一般强调神职人员与一般信徒（平信徒）的区别。
clergy 是天主教用得多的词，意思与 priest 接近。强调一个阶层。
preacher 也可以译为牧师，只是侧重点不同。此词从 preach 衍生，布道，宣讲神的信息。

A professional gambler
职业赌徒

A professional gambler

During **the Great Depression**, there was a man who walked into a bar one day. He went up to the bartender and said, "Bartender, I'd like to buy the house a round of drinks."

The bartender said, "That's fine, but we're in the middle of the Depression, so I'll need to see some money first."

The guy pulled out a huge wad of bills and set them on the bar. The bartender can't believe what he's seeing. "Where did you get all that money?" asked the bartender.

"I'm a **professional** gambler," replied the man.

The bartender said, "There's no such thing! I mean, your odds are fifty-fifty at best, right?"

"Well, I only bet on sure things," said the guy.

"Like what?" asked the bartender.

"Well, for example, I'll bet you fifty dollars that I can bite my right eye," he said.

The bartender thought about it. "Okay," he said.

So, the guy pulled out his false right eye and bit it. "Aw, you **screwed** me," said the bartender, and paid the guy his $50.

"I'll give you another chance. I'll bet you another fifty dollars that I can bite my left eye," said the stranger.

The bartender thought again and said, "Well, I know you're not blind, I mean, I watched you walk in here. I'll take that bet." So, the guy pulled out his false teeth and bit his left eye.

"Aw, you screwed me again!" protested the bartender.

"That's how I win so much money, bartender. I'll just take a bottle of your best scotch in lieu of the fifty dollars," said the man.

With that, the guy went to the back room and spent the better part of the night playing cards with some of the locals.

After many hours of drinking and card playing, he stumbled up to the bar. Drunk as a **skunk**, he said, "Bartender, I'll give you one last chance. I'll bet you five hundred dollars that I can stand on this bar on one foot and **piss** into that whiskey bottle on that shelf behind you without spilling a drop."

The bartender once again pondered the bet. The guy couldn't even stand up straight on two feet, much less one. "Okay, you're on," he said.

The guy climbed up on the bar, stood on one leg, and began pissing all over the place. He hit the bar, the bartender, himself, but not a drop made it into the whiskey bottle.

The bartender was **ecstatic**. Laughing, the bartender said, "Hey pal, you owe me five hundred dollars!"

The guy climbed down off the bar and said, "That's okay. I just bet each of the guys in the card room a thousand bucks each that I could piss all over you and the bar and still make you laugh!"

职业赌徒

经济大萧条时期。有一天，有个男人走进一家酒吧，对调酒师说："调酒师，我想为在座的所有客人每人买一杯酒。"

调酒师说："当然可以，不过现在正处于经济萧条时期，我需要先看到你带有足够的现金才行。"

那人从口袋里掏出一大迭钞票放到吧台上。调酒师简直不敢相信自己的眼睛，就问："你这些钱都是从哪儿弄来的？"

"我是一个职业赌徒。"男士回答。

"这不可能。我的意思是，在赌场你赢的机会最多也就五五开，不是吗？"调酒师说。

"那当然，不过我只打我必赢的赌。"男士说。

"比如呢？"调酒师问道。

"唔，例如，我可以和你赌 50 美元：我能够用自己的牙咬到自己的右眼睛。"他说。

调酒师想了一下，就说："那就来吧！"

于是，那个人将他右边的假眼抠了出来，用嘴咬了一下。

调酒师说声"靠！我上当了！"，就给了他 50 美元。

那陌生人又说道："我会再给你一次机会的。我再和你赌 50 美元：我可以用我的牙咬到我的左眼。"

调酒师想了想说道："哼！你又不是盲人，我的意思是说，我可是看着你走进这个酒吧的。这一把我和你赌定了！"

话刚出口，那家伙就从嘴里一把将假牙掰了下来，咬了左眼睛一下。

“靠！我又上当了！”调酒师几乎是抗议地叫出声来。

“这就是我赢了这么多钱的办法，小伙子！不过这次你也不用给我50元了，我只拿走一瓶威士忌就算了！”那人说道。

那个人拿了酒，就来到酒吧的后房，整个晚上的大部分时间都在和当地人打牌。

边喝边玩好几个小时之后，那个人又摇摇晃晃地来到吧台前，醉醺醺的样子，都快站不住了，他对调酒师说：“小伙子，我再给你最后一个机会。我和你赌500美元：我可以用一只脚站在这张吧台上撒尿，我能够把尿射到你身后酒架上的那个空瓶子里，而且保证不洒一滴到瓶子外边。”

调酒师再一次认真想了想：这家伙现在就是用两只脚都站不直，更别说用一条腿了……于是说：“好！那你就开始吧。”

只见那人爬到吧台上，来个金鸡独立，就开始撒尿。尿撒得到处都是：吧台上、调酒师身上和他自己身上，就是没有一滴尿到酒瓶里去。

小伙子简直开心死了，大笑着说：“老兄，这次你可欠我500块钱了。”

那家伙从吧台上爬了下来，说：“没问题。我刚和棋牌室里的每个人都赌了一千块钱，说我敢往你身上和吧台上撒尿，并且还能让你大笑！”

★★★★★

Two attorneys

Two **attorneys** went into a diner and ordered two drinks. Then they brought out sandwiches from their briefcases and started to eat. The owner **marched** over and told them，“You can't eat your own sandwiches here!”

The attorneys looked at each other，shrugged their shoulders and then **exchanged** sandwiches.

两个律师

两个律师走进一个餐厅点了两杯饮料，然后从手提箱中拿出三明治开始吃起来。餐厅老板走过来说道：“你们不能在这里吃自己的三明治。”

两个律师对看了一眼，耸耸肩，然后交换了手中的三明治。

实战提升
Practising
&
Exercise

单词 & 词组

professional [prə'feʃənl] *n.* 内行的，有经验的
screw over sb. 欺骗或玩弄（某人的）感情、金钱等
attorney [ə'tə:ni] *n.* 代理人，律师
skunk [skʌŋk] *n.* 讨厌鬼；使惨败
piss [pis] *n.* 小便
ecstatic [eks'tætik] *adj.* 狂喜的人；狂
march [mɑ:tʃ] *n.* 进军，行进；齐步走
exchange [iks'tʃeindʒ] *n.* 交换；交流

知道不知道

1929 年 10 月 29 日是美国历史上最黑暗的一天。“黑色星期二”是股票市场崩盘的日子，“经济大萧条”（Great Depression）也正式开始。失业率攀升到最高点。贺柏特·胡佛（Hebert Hoover）总统试图控制危机，但是却无能为力。1932 年，罗斯福获选为美国总统，他推动了“新政”（New Deal）以解决美国的经济危机。国会也配合通过设立“工作改进组织”（Works Progress Administration，WPA），负责为美国人民提供工作机会。美国于 1941 年加入第二次世界大战后，经济大萧条也随之结束。

How to refuse a boy
如何拒绝男孩

Boy：Can I buy you a drink？

Girl：Actually I'd rather have the money。

Boy：Can I have your name？

Girl：Why？ Don't you already have one？

Boy：I'm a **photographer**. I've been looking for a face like yours。

Girl：I'm a **plastic surgeon**. I've been looking for a face like yours。

Boy：Is this seat empty？

Girl：Yes，and this one will be if you sit down。

Boy：Haven't I seen you some place before？

Girl：Yes. That's why I don't go there anymore。

Boy：Will you go out with me this Saturday？

Girl：Sorry. I'm having a headache this weekend.

Boy：I think I could make you very happy。

Girl：Why？ Are you leaving？

Boy：May I hold your hand？

Girl：No thanks，it isn't heavy.

Boy：Hi，didn't we go on dates before？ Once or twice？

Girl：Must've been once.I never make the same mistake twice.

Boy：I'd like to call you. Your number？

Girl：It's in the phone book.

男孩：我可以为你买一杯饮料吗?

女孩：事实上，我更希望用钱。

男孩：可以告诉我你的名字吗？（直译：我能有你的名字吗？）

女孩：为什么？你不是已经有一个了吗？

男孩：我是摄影师。我一直在寻找一张像你这样的脸。

女孩：我是整形外科医生。我也一直在寻找一张像你这样的脸。

男孩：你旁边有人吗？（直译：这个座位是空的吧？）

女孩：是的，如果你坐下，我的座位就是空的。

男孩：我好象以前在什么地方见过你？

女孩：是的。这就是为什么我不再去那个地方的原因。

男孩：这个星期六你想跟我出去吗？

女孩：抱歉。这个周末我头疼。

男孩：我想我能让你非常快乐。

女孩：是吗？你是说你要离开？

男孩：我能牵着你的手吗？

女孩：不用了，我自己能拿的动。

男孩：我们以前有过一两次幽会吧

女孩：肯定只有一次，我从不会犯两次同样的错误。

男孩：能告诉我你的电话号码吗？

女孩：在电话本里。

男孩：这个位置没人吗？

女孩：对，即使你坐上去也是没人。

实战提升 Practising & Exercise

单词 & 词组

photographer [fə'tɔgrəfə] *n.* 摄影师

plastic surgeon 整形外科医生

知道不知道

如何拒绝男人其实还真不算新鲜话题了，幼儿园时，小女生被小男生追着跑时，会回家和大人告状说，“** 最坏了，老是欺负我，今天又拽着玩老鹰抓小鸡的游戏，还总让我当小鸡。”等上了高中，遇到不喜欢的男生搭讪，文静的女孩会说，“**，让我们做普通同学好么，希望你好好学习，努力考取心仪的大学。”彪悍的会说，“你究竟喜欢我哪一点，我改还不行吗？”等工作了成为社会人后，遇到不喜欢的男人，淑女会说，“我觉得我们还是更适合做普通朋友。”熟女会说，“我觉得你更适合做男朋友，而不适合当老公。”猛女会说，“不开 B 字头的车你也好意思来相亲啊。”（Bentley 宾利，宝马 BMW-Bayerische Motoren Werke，奔驰 Mercedes-Benz）别忘了还有我们的比亚迪（BYD-build your dream，意为成就你的梦想。）其实，做人也好，做事也好，都要明白努力不一定有结果，但心态要永远乐观向上，这才是你最大的心灵财富。

Women's words about marriage
女人婚后麻辣语录

At the **cocktail** party，one woman said to another，“Aren't you wearing your wedding ring on the wrong finger ? ” The other woman replied，“Yes，I am，I married the wrong man.”

在一个鸡尾酒舞会上，一个女人对另外一个女人说：“你的结婚戒指带错手指了。”
另一个回答说：“是的，人也嫁错了。”

★★★★★

When a woman steals your husband，there is no better **revenge** than to let her keep him.

如果一个女人偷了你的老公，最好的复仇方式便是让她继续拥有他。

★★★★★

Eighty percent of married men cheat in the U.S.A. The rest cheat in Canada.
在美国 80% 的已婚男人撒谎，其余的 20% 在加拿大撒谎。

★★★★★

A woman is **incomplete** until she is married. Then she is finished.
女人要到结婚时才算完整，结婚后便完蛋了。

★★★★★

Then there was a woman who said, "I never knew what real happiness was until I got married; and by then it was too late."

有女人曾说："直至结婚了，我才晓得真正的快乐是什么，但是已经太晚了。"

★★★★★

Marriage is the **triumph** of imagination over intelligence.
婚姻便是想象力战胜智力的成功案例。

实战提升 Practising & Exercise

单词 & 词组

cocktail ['kɔkteil] *n.* 鸡尾酒

revenge [ri'vendʒ] *n.* 报仇，报复

incomplete [ˌinkəm'pliːt] *adj.* 不完全的，未完成的

triumph ['traiəmf] *n.* 胜利，成功

知道不知道

幸福的秘密

要想与一个男人幸福地相守，你必须对他多一份理解少一份爱。(To be happy with a man，you must understand him a lot and love him a little.)

要想与一个女人幸福地生活，你必须尽量多爱她，而绝不要试图理解她。(To be happy with a woman，you must love her a lot and not try to understand her at all.)

All in the same boat
同舟共济

A good boy

Little Robert asked his mother for two cents. “What did you do with the money I gave you yesterday ? ”

“I gave it to a poor old woman.” he answered.

“You're a good boy,” said the mother proudly. “Here are two cents more. But why are you so interested in the old woman ? ”

“She is the one who sells the candy.”

好孩子

小罗伯特向妈妈要两分钱。

“昨天给你的钱干什么了? ”

“我给了一个可怜的老太婆。”他回答说。“你真是个好孩子,”妈妈骄傲地说,“再给你两分钱。可你为什么对那位老太太那么感兴趣呢? ”

“她是个卖糖果的。”

★★★★★

They're **all in the same boat**

Three men were sitting on a bench in the park. The middle one was reading a newspaper, and the others were pretending to fish. They **baited** imaginary hooks, cast **lines** and **reeled** in their catch. A passing policeman stopped to watch the spectacle and asked the man in the middle if he knew the other two. "Oh, yes, they're my friends!" "In that case," the police officer warned him, "you had better get them out of here." "Yes, Sir!" the man replied, andhe began **rowing furiously**.

同舟共济

有三个男人坐在公园的长椅上，中间那位在看报纸，另外两位则假装在钓鱼，他们用假想的鱼钩挂饵、抛出钓鱼线，再收线拉回他们钓到的东西。一位警察路过这里，他停下来看着这奇怪的一幕，然后问中间这个人是否认识其他两位。“喔，是的，他们是我的朋友！”警察于是警告他说：“既然如此，你最好把他们带走。”他回答：“是，警察先生！”然后开始奋力地划船。

实战提升
Practising & Exercise

单词 & 词组

all in the same boat 字面意思是：大家都在同一条船上，指处境相同、面对同样困难或危险的人，他们的命运也会相同。

bait [beit] *n.*（钓鱼等用的）饵，诱饵；装饵

line [lain] *n.* 线；皱纹；行

reel [riːl] *n.* 把东西用卷轴卷起来

row [rau] *v.* 划船；争吵，吵闹

furiously ['fjuəriəsli] *adv.* 狂怒地；猛烈地

知道不知道

boat, vessel, ship, craft 有何区别

这几个词都有"船"的意思。boat 指小船，如用桨划行的船、帆船或小机动船。

ship 指航海的大船，如大帆船、轮船、战船等。ship 能用于比喻，可以用于文学语言。vessel 从词源学角度看指的是容器，在用来表示船只时，尤指运载货物或乘客的航海大船。craft 既可用于单数概念，也可用于复数概念，用作集体名词，表示一切的 boats 和 vessels。

This is my first operation
这也是我第一次动手术

My first operation

Patient：I'm so **frightened**，this is my first operation.

Surgeon：I know just how you feel. This is my first operation，too.

这也是我第一次动手术

病人：我很害怕，这是我第一次动手术。

外科医生：我完全理解你的心情。这也是我第一次动手术。

★★★★★

Don't be selfIsh

A mother is **admonishing** her son.

"Now，John，don't be selfish. Let your little brother share the bicycle with you."

"But Mother，I do. I ride it down the hill，and he rides it up the hill."

别太自私

一位母亲在劝告她的儿子。

"听着，约翰，别太自私，让你弟弟和你共用一辆自行车。"

"妈妈，我是让他。我先骑下坡，他再骑上坡。"

★★★★★

Hospitality

The **hostess** apologized to her unexpected guest for serving an applepie without any cheese. The little boy of the family left the room quietly for a moment and returned with a piece of cheese which he laid on the guest's plate. The visitor smiled, put the cheese into his mouth and then said: "You must have better eyes than your mother, sonny. Where did you find the cheese?" "In the **rat-trap**, sir." replied the boy.

好客

客人在吃苹果馅饼时，家里没有奶酪了，于是女主人向大家表示歉意。这家的小男孩悄悄地离开了屋子。过了一会儿，他拿着一片奶酪回到房间，把奶酪放在客人的盘子里。客人微笑着把奶酪放进嘴里说："孩子，你的眼睛就是比你妈妈的好。你在哪里找到的奶酪？"

"在捕鼠夹上，先生。"小男孩说。

★★★★★

Always thirsty

"I had an operation," said a man to his friend, "and the doctor left a **sponge** in me."

"That's terrible!" said the friend. "Got any pain?"

"No, but I am always thirsty!"

总感到口渴

一个男人对他的朋友说："我动了一次手术，手术后医生把一块海绵忘在我的身体里了。"

"真是太糟糕了！"朋友说道："你觉得疼吗？"

"不疼，可是我总感到口渴。"

★★★★★

A businessman enters a **tavern**, sits down at the bar, and orders a double martini **on the rocks**.

After he finishes the drink, he **peeks** inside his shirt pocket, and then orders the bartender to prepare another double martini.

After he finishes that, he again peeks inside his shirt pocket and orders the bartender to bring another double martini.

The bartender says," Look, buddy, I'll bring ya'martinis all night long – but you gotta tell me why you look inside your shirt pocket before you order a refill."

The customer replies," I'm peeking at a photo of my wife. When she starts to look good, I know it's time to go home."

一个生意人走进一家酒馆，在吧台坐下，点了一杯加冰的双料马提尼酒。

喝完，那生意人往自己衬衣的口袋里瞥了一眼，然后又让服务员把杯子满上。

喝完，生意人又往自己衬衣的口袋里瞥了一眼，然后又让服务生帮他把杯子倒满。

这时酒馆的服务生说话了，“哦，老兄，我整个晚上给你倒马提尼都没有问题，但你得告诉我，你为什么在点下一杯酒前都要往自己衬衣的口袋里偷偷看那么一眼呢。”

这位客人回答道，“我看的是我老婆的一张照片。如果照片上的人开始变得好看起来，那就说明我喝得差不多了，该回家了。”

实战提升 Practising & Exercise

单词 & 词组

frightened ['frait(ə)nd] *adj.* 受惊的，害怕的

admonish [əd'mɔniʃ] *vt.* 劝告，训诫

hospitality [ˌhɔspi'tæliti] *n.* 殷勤，好客

hostess ['həustis] *n.* 女主人

rat-trap 捕鼠器

sponge [spʌndʒ] *n.* 海绵

tavern ['tævə(ː)n] *n.* 小旅馆，酒馆

on the rocks 触礁，搁浅，加冰块

peek [piːk] *n.* 一瞥，匆忙看

知道不知道

世界十大鸡尾酒

1. 玛格丽特 (Margarita)
2. 椰林飘香 (Pina Colada)
3. 新加坡司令 (Singapore Sling)
4. 蓝色夏威夷 (Blue Hawaii)
5. 海岸 (Sex on the Beach)
6. 干马提尼 (Dry Martini)
7. 周游世界 (Around World)
8. 莫斯科骡子 (Moscow Mule)
9. 生锈钉 (Rusty Nail)
10. 咸狗 (Salty Dog)

Bad acting has its benefits
演技三流有好处

A young businessman had just started his own firm. He rented a beautiful office and had it furnished with antiques. Sitting there, he saw a man come in to the outer office. Wishing to appear the hot shot, the businessman picked up the phone and started to pretend he had a big deal working. He threw huge figures around and made giant commitments. Finally he hung up and asked the visitor, "Can I help you？" The man said, "Yeah, I've come to **activate** your phone lines."

一个年轻人的公司刚刚开张。他租用了漂亮的办公室，还在办公室里放了古董作装饰。

一天，这位年轻人正在办公室里面坐着，他看到一个男的走进了办公室。为显示他是个成功的老板，这位年轻人拿起电话假装正在谈大买卖，开口就是高价。

最后，他挂上听筒后问进来的那个人："您有事吗?"那人说，"有事，我是来给你开通电话的"。

★★★★★

Bad acting has its benefits

There once was a young man who went to his girlfriend's house and said to her father, "Sir, may I ask your permission to marry your daughter?" And the father said, "No way. There's no way my daughter is going to marry an actor. That's final!" But the boy begged him, "Please, before you make a final decision, would you at least go to see me perform tonight and then decide?" So the father said, "OK, fair enough."

So that evening the father took his daughter to the theater to see the young man perform, and after the performance, he took his daughter backstage into the young man's dressing room and said, "OK, you can marry my daughter, no problem." The young man was beside himself and so happy that he said, "Yes, sir, but why?" And the father said, "Because you're no actor."

演技三流有好处

有一个年轻人到他女朋友家，对女友的父亲说："伯父，请您把女儿嫁给我好吗？"女孩的父亲回答："不！我女儿绝不能嫁给一个演员，不用再说了！"但是男孩请求他说："拜托您至少先看了我今晚的表演，再做最后决定好吗？"那位父亲说："好吧！这要求不过分。"

当天晚上，这位父亲就带着女儿去剧院看年轻人的演出。表演结束后，他带女儿到后台的演员化妆室，告诉年轻人说："没问题，你可以娶我的女儿。"年轻人欣喜若狂地说："太好了！是什么原因让您同意呢？"这位父亲回答："因为你不是当演员的料！"

★★★★★

Sweet revenge

A grandmother gave a water pistol as a birthday gift to her grandson. So he was squeezing and **squashing** it everywhere, **splashing** all over, and the mother was very, very **disturbed**.

She looked **sternly** at her own mother, the grandmother. "I'm surprised at you, mother!"

"Why?" "Don't you remember how we used to drive you crazy with water guns?"

The grandmother said, "Yes dear, I remember!"

甜蜜的报复

外婆送给孙子一枝玩具水枪作为生日礼物。结果孙子拿着水枪玩耍，喷得到处都是水，让妈妈非常生气。

她板着脸看着自己的母亲说道："妈，您让我感到很诧异！""怎么啦？""您不记得以前我们是如何用水枪让您抓狂的吗？""亲爱的，我记得啊！"

★★★★★

A holiday from school

Tommy hated school and was always looking for excuses not to go.

If he sneezed, he asked his mother to write a note saying he had a cold.

If he had a headache, he asked his mother to take him to the doctor during school hours.

He spent more time at home than he did at school.

On the days that he did go to school, he looked for excuses to come home early.

One morning he came home when the lessons were only half finished.

His father was surprised.

"You've come home early," he said. "Is the school closed today?"

"No, Dad", Tommy said, "It's open. I came home early."

"How did you do that? his father asked him. "What did you say to the teacher?"

"I told her that I had a new baby brother and that I had to come home and help you."

"But your mother has had twins," his father said, "a boy and a girl. You've got a baby brother and a baby sister."

"Yes, I know, Dad," Tommy said. "I'm saving up my baby sister for next week."

休假

汤姆讨厌上学，总是找借口不去上学.

如果他打喷嚏，他就叫他妈妈写个纸条说他感冒了。

如果他头痛，他就叫他妈妈在上课时间带他去看病。

他呆在家里的时间比在学校的时间要多。

在他的确去上学的日子里，他就找借口早点回家。

一天早上他上了一半课就从学校回来了。

他爸爸很惊讶。

"你回来得很早，"他爸爸问，"学校放学了吗?"

"没有，爸爸，"汤姆说，"还没放学。我提前回来了。"

"你怎么会提前回来了?"爸爸问，"你对老师说什么了?"

"我告诉她我有了一个小弟弟，我得回家帮你。"

"但是你妈妈生了一对双胞胎，"爸爸说，"一个男孩，一个女孩。你有一个小弟弟和一个小妹妹。"

"是的，我知道，爸爸，"汤姆说，"我要等下个星期再说我有个小妹妹了。"

★★★★★

What time is it now ?

The two boys were **camping** in the backyard. When they couldn't figure out what time it was, the first boy said to the second, "Start singing very loud."

"How will that help ? " said the second boy.

"Just do it," insisted the first.

Both boys broke into song, singing at the top of their lungs. Moments later, a neighbor threw open her window and shouted, "Keep it down! Don't you know it's three o'clock in the morning ? "

现在几点了?

两个男孩子在后院露营，他们不知道那会儿是晚上几点钟。于是，一个男孩对另外一个说："我们大声唱歌就行了。"

"那样就会知道是几点吗?" 第二个男孩问。

"只管唱吧。" 第一个坚持道。

两个孩子开始大声唱歌，过了一会儿，一个邻居打开窗户喊道："小声点！你们不知道现在是凌晨三点吗?"

实战提升
Practising & Exercise

单词 & 词组

activate ['æktiveit] *vt.* 激活，起动
squash [skwɔʃ] *v.* 挤压，压扁
splash [splæʃ] *n.* 溅泼，溅落
disturbed [dis'tə:bd] *adj.* 扰乱的
sternly ['stɜnli] *adv.* 严格地，坚决地
camp [kæmp] *vt.* 营地，露营

知道不知道

revenge 和 avenge 有何区别

这两个词都表示“复仇”之意，但词义和使用场合有所不同。revenge 大都指为自己报仇，有时它还带有报复的意味。Avenge 大都指替别人复仇，复仇的动机并不是为了自己，而是为了正义感。

Columbus' telephone number
哥伦布的电话号码

Five hundred times

In the traffic **court** of a large mid-western city, a young lady was brought before the judge to answer a ticket given her for driving through a red light. She explained to his honor that she was a school teacher and requested an immediate disposal of her case in order that she might hasten on to her classes. A wild **gleam** came into the judge's eye. "You are a school teacher, eh ?" said he. "Madam, I shall realize my lifelong **ambition**. Sit down at that table and write 'I went through a red light' five hundred times."

五百遍

在中西部一个大城市的交通法庭里，一位年轻女士被带到法官面前，她由于开车闯红灯被开了罚单。女士向法官解释，她是一名学校老师，请求法官马上处理她的案子，以便可以赶回去上课。法官眼中闪过一丝狡黠，说道："你是学校的老师，对吗？女士，我马上要实现我毕生的愿望了。到那张桌子旁坐下，写'我开车闯了红灯'500遍。"

★★★★★

Leading questions

Teacher：Billy，What does C–A–T Spell？

Billy：Don't know，sir.

Teacher：What does your mother keep to catch mice？

Billy：A trap，sir.

Teacher：No. What animal is fond of milk？

Billy：The baby，sir.

Teacher：You stupid! What was it that scratched your sister's face？

Billy：My nails，sir.

Teacher：You're putting me out of patience! Do you see that animal in the yard？ then tell me，what does C–A–T spell？

Billy：**Kitten**，sir.

诱导性的提问

老师：比利，C–A–T 拼出来是什么词?

比利：不知道，先生。

老师：你妈妈用什么逮老鼠?

比利：捕鼠夹，先生。

老师：不对，不对。什么动物非常喜欢喝牛奶?

比利：婴儿，先生。

老师：你真笨！是什么东西抓破了你妹妹的脸?

比利：我的指甲，先生。

老师：你真叫我生气！你看院子里是什么动物? 告诉我，C–A–T 拼出来是什么字?

比利：Kitten（小猫），先生。

★★★★★

Columbus' telephone number

Little Mary：I find in my history book there is always such

number（1451—1560）after the name Christopher Columbus. Would you please explain why，sir？
Little Rose：I can tell her，sir. It was Columbus' telephone number.

哥伦布的电话号码
小玛丽：我在历史书中发现，克里斯托弗·哥伦布这个名字后面老是有（1451–1560）这几个数字，老师，请您给解释一下好吗？
小罗斯：老师，我知道。那是哥伦布的电话号码。

★★★★★

I'm glad

A **Sunday-school** teacher was telling her pupils the importance of making others glad. "Now，children，" she said，"has anyone of you ever made someone else glad？"
"Please，teacher，" said a small boy，"I've make someone glad yesterday."
"Well done. Who was that!"
"My granny."
"Good boy. Now tell us how you made your grandmother glad."
"Please，teacher，I went to see her yesterday，and stayed with her three hours. Then I said to her，'Granny，I'm going home.' and she said，'Well，I'm glad'！"

我很高兴
一个主日学校的教师正在对学生讲让别人高兴的重要性。"听着，孩子们，"她说，"你们当中有谁曾让别人高兴过吗？"
"我，老师，"一个小男孩说，"昨天我就让别人高兴过。"
"做得好，是谁呢？"
"我奶奶。"

“好孩子。告诉我们，你是怎样使你奶奶高兴的？”
“是这样的，老师。昨天我去看她，在她那儿待了三个小时。然后我对她说‘奶奶，我要回家了。’她说‘啊，我很高兴！’”

★★★★★

An abstract drawing

One day in a drawing class，the teacher told the class to draw an abstract drawing.

After a while，a small boy turned his drawing in. The teacher looked at it but saw nothing，only a piece of white paper.

“What did you draw？” said the teacher.

“A cow eats grass，” the boy answered.

“Where is the grass？”

“The cow has eaten it up.” replied the boy.

“Well，but where is the cow？” the teacher asked again.

“It ate up the grass and then went away to drink water.”

一幅抽象画

美术课上，老师要同学们画一幅抽象画。

一会儿工夫，一个小男孩交了他的作品，老师看了看，上面什么也没有，只不过是一张白纸。

“你画的是什么呀？”老师说。

“牛吃草。”孩子答道。

“草呢？”

“牛把它吃光了。”孩子说。

“那么，牛在哪儿呢？”老师又问。

“吃完草，牛便喝水去了。”

实战提升 Practising & Exercise

单词 & 词组

court [kɔːt] *n.* 法庭，法院

gleam [gliːm] *vi.*（感情的）表露，闪现

ambition [æm'biʃən] *n.* 追求的目标，夙愿

kitten ['kitn] *n.* 小猫

sunday school 主日学校（基督教堂或犹太教堂在星期日为儿童提供宗教教育）

知道不知道

相关美术词汇一览

水粉画 opaque watercolour painting
水墨画 Chinese brush drawing
水彩画 watercolor painting
毛笔画 brush drawing
国画 Chinese painting
油画 oil painting
工笔画 claborate-style painting
蜡笔画 pastel drawing
版画 engraving
临摹 tracing
草稿 sketch

4-4 =?
四减四等于几?

Lady first

A teacher asked her class: "Is the sentence 'The **ox** and the **cow** are in the fields' correct?"

Most of the children said: "Yes, it is all right!"

And only one little boy said: "No, it is not correct. The lady must be mentioned first."

女士优先

一位老师问班上的学生:"公牛和母牛在田里"这个句子对吗?"

大多数学生回答说:"对,一点不错。"

只有一个小男孩说:"不对,应该先说女士。"

★★★★★

The biggest in the world

Peter dozed off while his teacher was talking.

Teacher: Peter! Tell us, what's the biggest in the world?

Peter: Well, well... **eyelids**...

Teacher: What? Eyelids?

Peter: Yes, sir. Because as soon as I shut my eyes, the eyelids cover everything of the world.

世界上最大的

老师正在讲课，彼得打起瞌睡来了。

老师：彼得！你说说，世界上什么最大？

彼得：这，这……眼皮……

老师：什么？眼皮？

彼得：是这样，老师，因为只要我闭上眼睛，眼皮就把世界上的一切东西都遮住了。

★★★★★

Father's John Hancock

Teacher：Tom，you haven't shown your parents the examination papers，have you？

Tom：Yes，I have，sir.

Teacher：But I can't find your father's **John Hancock** on the papers at all.

Tom：Here，sir.（showing his whipped arms to the teacher.）

父亲的亲笔签名

老师：汤姆，你没把你的考卷给你父母看，对吗？

汤姆：不，老师，我给他们看了。

老师：可是我在上面根本没找着你父亲的亲笔签名啊。

汤姆：在这里，老师。（向老师展示手臂上的鞭伤）

★★★★★

4−4=？

One day，the teacher inquired Peter：“How much is four **minus** four？” Peter was tongue-tied.

The teacher got angry and said：“What a fool! You see，if I put four coins in your pocket，but there is a hole in your pocket and all of them **leak out**，now what is left in your pocket？"

"The hole." replied Peter.

四减四等于几?

一天，老师问彼得："4减4等于几?"彼得张口结舌答不上来。

老师生气地说："真笨！比如我给你衣袋里装进4个硬币，可你衣袋上有个窟窿，硬币全从这里漏掉了，那么，你衣袋里还剩下什么?"

"还剩下个窟窿。"彼得答道。

★★★★★

A problem in arithmetic

Bill is a good student and an intelligent boy. He likes to study **arithmetic**，and he can do all of the arithmetic problems in his book easily.

One day on his way to school Bill passed a fruit store. There was a sign in the window which said，"Apple–Six for five cents." An idea came to Bill and he went into the store.

"How much are the apples？" he asked the store.

"Six for five cents."

"But I don't want six apples."

"How many apples do you want？"

"It is not a question of how many apples I want. It is a problem in arithmetic."

"What do you mean by a problem in arithmetic？" asked the man.

"Well，if six apples are worth five cents，then five apples are worth four cents，four apples are worth three cents，three apples are worth two cents，two apples are worth one cent and one apple is worth nothing. I only want one apple, and if one apple is worth nothing then it is not necessary for me to pay you."

Bill picked out a good apple, began to eat it, and walked happily out of the store. The man looked at the young boy with such surprise that he could not say a word.

一个数学问题

比尔是一个好学生，也是个聪明的孩子。他喜欢学数学，课本上所有的数学问题他都能不费劲地解答。

有一天，在上学路上，比尔经过一家水果店。该店窗户上有个招牌上写着："苹果——五美分六个。"比尔脑筋一转，进了店门。

"苹果怎么卖？"

"五美分六个。"

"但我不想要六个。"

"你想要几个？"

"这不是我想要几个的问题。这是个数学问题。"

"数学问题？你说这话是什么意思？"

"你看，如果六个苹果五美分，那么五个苹果四美分，四个苹果三美分，三个苹果二美分，二个苹果一美分，一个苹果就不要钱。我只要一个苹果，如果一个苹果一分钱也不要的话，那我也就没必要给你钱了。"

比尔拣了一个好苹果，开始吃了起来，然后兴高采烈地迈出了店门。那个售货员吃惊地望着这个小男孩，一句话也说不出来。

实战提升 Practising & Exercise

单词 & 词组

ox [ɔks] *n.* 公牛
cow [kau] *n.* 母牛
eyelid ['ailid] *n.* 眼睑
John Hancock 亲笔签名
minus ['mainəs] *adj.*（表示运算）减去，符号
leak out 漏出，渗出，泄露
arithmetic [ə'riθmətik] *n.* 算术，计算

知道不知道

John Hancock 为什么会有"亲笔签名"的含义?

原来在历史上，John Hancock 是一个真实存在的人，是美国独立宣言中第一个签署的人。因为他在宣言上的签名特别明显，所以英文中的 John Hancock 就成了亲笔签名的代名词。所以，如果有人对你说 Please put your John Hancock at the bottom of the paper 的话，那就是请你在文件上留下亲笔签名哦。

If I am a manager
如果我是一名经理

The reason of being late

Teacher：Johnny，why are you late for school every morning？

Johnny：Every time I come to the corner，a **guidepost** says，'School — Go Slow' .

迟到的原因

老师：约翰尼，为什么你每天早晨都迟到?

约翰尼：每次我经过学校附近的拐角处，就见路牌上写着'学校——缓行'。

★★★★★

It's kind of fitting

As a freshman at the University of Dayton in Ohio，I was eager to make a good impression on my new roommate. When I arrived at our dorm room，I found her putting on **perfume**. "That's a great scent，" I said，making conversation.

"Thanks–it was from my boyfriend. Here，try some，" she said，holding the bottle out for me.

Unfortunately she let go before I had a firm **grip**，and the glass shattered on the tile floor. Embarrassed, I tried to apologize, but she cut me off – "Actually, **it's kind of fitting**," she explained, surveying the damage. "That's exactly how the relationship went."

理应如此

作为俄亥俄州代顿大学的一名新生，我急于给我的新舍友留个好印象。我到了寝室，看到她正在往身上洒香水。"这香味真棒啊。"我说，想和她搭起话来。

"谢谢——是男朋友送的，来，洒些试试。"她说着把瓶子递给我。不幸的是，我还没抓牢她就松手了，玻璃瓶在瓷砖地板上摔碎了。我感到很窘，刚想道歉，她就打断了我。"事实上，应该如此。"她解释道，一边审视着地上的碎渣，"我和他的关系正是这样的。"

★★★★★

Kate: Mom, do you know what I'm going to give you for your birthday?

Mom: No, Honey, what?

Kate: A nice teapot.

Mom: But I've got a nice teapot.

Kate: No, you haven't. I've just dropped it.

凯特：妈妈，你知道我要送你一件什么生日礼物吗?

妈妈：不知道，宝贝，是什么呀?

凯特：一把漂亮的茶壶。

妈妈：可是我已经有一把漂亮的茶壶了呀。

凯特：不，你没有。我刚刚把它给摔坏了。

★★★★★

whose father was the stronger

Will and Bill were quarrelling about whose father was the stronger. Will said, "Well, you know the Pacific Ocean？ My father's the one who dug the hole for it."
Bill wasn't impressed, "Well, that's nothing. You know the Dead Sea？ My father's the one who killed it!"

谁的爸爸是最强壮的

维尔和比尔为谁的爸爸更强壮而争吵不休。维尔说："你知道太平洋吗？那个坑是我爸爸挖的。"
比尔不屑地说："那没什么。你知道死海吗？那是我爸爸打死的。"

★★★★★

If I am a manager

One day in class, the teacher **assigned** his students to write a **composition** - If I Am a Manager.
All the students began to write except a boy. The teacher went to him and asked the reason.
"I am waiting for my **secretary**," was the boy's answer.

如果我是一名经理

有一天在课堂上，老师要同学们以"如果我是一名经理"为题写一篇作文。
所有的学生都在动笔写了，只有一个男生例外。老师走过去问他为什么不写。
"我在等我的秘书"，男生答道。

实战提升 Practising & Exercise

单词 & 词组

guidepost ['gaɪdpəʊst] *n.* 路标，路牌

perfume ['pəːfjuːm] *n.* 香味，芳香，香水

grip [grip] *n.* 紧握，紧夹

It's kind of fitting. 理应如此。

assign [ə'sain] *vt.* 分配，指派

composition [kɔmpə'ziʃən] *n.* 写作，作文，成分，合成物

secretary ['sekrətri] *n.* 秘书，书记，部长，大臣

知道不知道

a dead sea apple=apple of Sodom，源自《圣约·旧约·创世纪》。据载，所多玛（Sodom）是古代死海（Dead Sea）附近的城市。由于那里的居民罪孽深重，上帝降天火焚毁所多玛后，在焦土上长出了苹果树，结出的果子外观诱人，但一摘就冒烟成灰。所以，apple of Sodom 就被用来喻指“华而不实，徒有虚表的东西”。

Where is the father？
父亲在哪儿？

Two birds

Teacher：Here are two birds，one is a **swallow**，the other is a **sparrow**. Now who can tell us which is which？

Student：I cannot point out but I know the answer.

Teacher：Please tell us.

Student：The swallow is beside the sparrow and the sparrow is beside the swallow.

两只鸟

老师：这儿有两只鸟，一只是燕子，另一只是麻雀。谁能指出哪只是燕子，哪只是麻雀吗？

学生：我指不出，但我知道答案。

老师：请说说看。

学生：燕子旁边的就是麻雀，麻雀旁边的就是燕子。

★★★★★

Give me a dollar

Son：Dad，give me a **dime**.

Father：Son，don't you think you're getting too big to be forever begging for dimes ?

Son：I guess you're right，Dad，give me a dollar，will you ?

给我一块钱

儿子：爸爸，给我一角钱。

父亲：儿子，你不认为你已经长大了，不该再老是一角一角地要钱了吗?

儿子：爸爸，我想你是对的，那给我一块钱行吗?

★★★★★

Mixed doubles

Teacher of Physical Education：Have you ever seen **mixed doubles**，boys ?

Nick：Yes，sir. Quite often. I saw it even last night.

Teacher：Please tell us something about it.

Nick：Oh，sorry，sir. My father always says，'**Domestic shame should not be published.**'

混合双打

体育老师：孩子们，你们见过男女混合双打吗?

尼克：见过，老师，经常见。就在昨天夜里我还见过呢。

老师：你给大家讲讲当时的情形吧。

尼克：啊，对不起，老师。我爸爸常说，"家丑不可外扬。"

★★★★★

Saving a dollar

Johnny：Papa，would you be glad if I saved a dollar for you ?

Papa：Naturally，my son.

Johnny：Well，I have saved one dollar for you. You said that if I brought a good mark this week, you would give me a dollar and I haven't brought one.

省下一美元

Johnny：爸爸，如果我为你省下一美元，你高兴不？

Papa：当然啦，孩子！

Johnny：那好，我省下一美元了。你说过我这个礼拜考出好成绩，就会给我一美元。我没考好！

★★★★★

Jim's history examination

Aunt：How did Jim do his history examination？

Mother：Oh，not at all well，but there，it wasn't his fault. Why，they asked him things that happened before the poor boy was born.

吉姆的历史考试

姨妈：吉姆这孩子历史考得怎么样？

母亲：唉，糟透了。可话又说回来，这也不能怪他。嗨，他们尽问些这个可怜的孩子出生前的事情。

★★★★★

Where is the father？

Two brothers were looking at some beautiful paintings.

"Look，" said the elder brother. "How nice these paintings are!"

"Yes，" said the younger，"but in all these paintings there is only the mother and the children. Where is the father？"

The elder brother thought for a moment and then explained，"Obviously he was painting the pictures."

父亲在哪儿?

兄弟俩在看一些漂亮的油画。

“看,”哥哥说,“这些画多漂亮呀!”

“是啊,”弟弟说道,“可是在所有这些画中,只有妈妈和孩子。那爸爸去哪儿了呢?”

哥哥想了会儿,然后解释道:“很明显,他当时正在画这些画呗。”

★★★★★

实战提升

Practising & Exercise

单词 & 词组

swallow ['swɔləu] *n.* 燕子，吞咽，喉

sparrow ['spærəu] *n.* 雀；麻雀

dime [daim] *n.* 一角硬币

mixed doubles 混合双打

domestic shame should not be published. 家丑不可外扬

知道不知道

常用俗语

Good health is over wealth. 健康是最大的财富。

Honesty is the best policy. 做人诚信为本。

A bad workman always blames his tools. 不会撑船怪河弯。

A bird in the hand is worth than two in the bush. 一鸟在手胜过双鸟在林。

A bad thing never dies. 遗臭万年。

A good beginning makes a good ending. 善始者善终。

A good book is a good friend. 好书如挚友。

A good medicine tastes bitter. 良药苦口。

A hedge between keeps friendship green. 君子之交淡如水。

All rivers run into sea. 海纳百川。All roads lead to Rome. 条条大路通罗马。

All that ends well is well. 结果好，就一切都好。

An apple a day keeps the doctor away. 一天一苹果，医生远离我。

Logical thinking
逻辑思维

She ate all my bait

The young boy protested **vigorously** when his mother asked him to take his little sister along fishing. "The last time she came," he objected, "I didn't catch a single fish."

"I'll talk to her," his mother said, "and I promise this time she won't make any noise."

"It wasn't the noise, Mom," the boy replied. "She ate all my **bait**."

她把所有的诱饵都吃了

妈妈提出让小男孩带着妹妹一起去钓鱼时，他坚决反对。"上次她跟着我，"他抗议道："我连一条鱼都没能钓上。"

"我会告诉她，"妈妈说，"我保证这次她不会吵闹了。"

"妈妈，不是吵闹，"男孩回答，"是她把所有的诱饵都吃了。"

★★★★★

The result of a promise

Father：I promised to buy you a car if you passed your examination, and you have failed. What were you doing last term？

Son：I was learning to drive a car.

许诺的结果

父亲：我曾许诺说，如果你考试及格就给你买辆小汽车，可你却没通过考试。你上学期一直在干什么呀?

儿子：我在学开汽车。

★★★★★

logical thinking

The teacher told the class the story of a man who swam a river three times before breakfast.

Johnny laughed.

"Do you **doubt** that a good swimmer could do that ? " asked the teacher.

"No，sir，" answered Johnny，"but I wonder why he did not swim it four times and get back to the side where his clothes were."

逻辑思维

老师给同学们讲了一个小故事，说有一个人早饭前要在河里游泳，横渡三趟。

约翰尼笑了。

老师问："你不相信游泳很好的人可以做到这个? "

约翰尼回答说："不，我相信，但我不明白他为什么不游四次，好回到他放衣服的那边呢。"

★★★★★

Go barefoot

In secondary school，I was always **self-conscious** about my height.

Once I was asked out by a life-guard. I had never really stood next to him and didn't know how tall he was, so the night of the date I took out two pairs of shoes–one with heels, one flat. I arranged with my brother to answer the door, compare his height with my date's and run upstairs to let me know which shoes to wear.

When the doorbell rang I waited. Then my brother showed up and told me what I didn't want to hear: "Go **barefoot**."

光着脚去约会

念中学的时候，我对自己的身高非常敏感。

一次，一位救生员约我出去。事实上，我从未和他并肩站过，因而不知道他到底有多高。因此约会那晚，我拿出两双鞋，一双高跟，一双平跟。我安排哥哥去开门，让他和救生员比比高度，再上楼告诉我应穿哪双鞋。

门铃响了，我在楼上等着。哥哥跑上楼告诉了我一个不幸的消息："你可以光着脚去约会。"

★★★★★

Homework

Teacher: I'm able to read one of the essays you did for homework, but the other one is written very poorly.

Student: Yes, sir — my mother is a much better writer than my father.

家庭作业

老师：我只能读通你的一篇作文，可另一篇实在是糟透了。

学生：是的，先生——我妈妈的文采要比我爸爸的好多了。

★★★★★

实战提升 Practising & Exercise

单词 & 词组

vigorously ['vigərəsli] *adv.* 精神旺盛地
bait [beit] *n.* 饵，诱惑物
doubt [daut] *n.* 怀疑，疑惑，疑问
self-conscious 自觉的；自知的
barefoot ['beəfut] *adj.* 赤脚的

知道不知道

appointment 与 date 的区别

appointment 是预约，名词，常见表达 make an appointment，意思是与某人有预约。date 是约会，date 还可以做动词，表示和某人约会。

Those funny words
经典搞笑雷人语录

◎ My **advantage** is that I am handsome，but my **disadvantage** is that the handsomeness is not so obvious.
我的优点是：我很帅，我的缺点是：我帅的不够明显。

◎ I **curse** your buying instant noodles without getting **flavoring** bags.
我诅咒你买方便面没有调料包。

◎ When I went shopping one day，a group of girls stopped me，saying that I was handsome. But I denied it，and then they hit me and said I am **hypocritical**.
有一次我购物时，一群女孩把我拦住，她们说我帅，我不承认，她们就打我，还说我虚伪。

◎ There are two things that I could not do in my life – I could not do this and I could not do that.
我这辈子只有两件事不会：这也不会，那也不会。

◎ Never treat a dried shrimp not as seafood.
别把虾米不当海鲜。

◎ I am an angel, and the reason why I can not go back to heaven is the problem of my weight.
我是天使，回不去天堂是因为体重的原因。

◎ Since there are so many **deceivers**, it is very obvious that idiots are not enough.
骗子太多，傻子明显不够用了。

◎ Your phone is much cheaper than the phone words fee.
你的手机比话费还便宜。

★★★★★

Perfect match

A wealthy **matron** is so proud of a valuable **antique** vase that she decides to have her bedroom painted the same color as the vase. Several painters try to match the shade, but none comes close enough to satisfy the **eccentric** woman.

Eventually, a painter approaches who is confident he can mix the proper color. The woman is pleased with the result, and the painter becomes famous.

Years later, he retires and turns the business over to his son. "Dad," says the son, "there's something I've got to know. How did you get those walls to match the vase so perfectly ? "

"Son," the father replies , "I painted the vase."

绝配

一位富婆为拥有一只珍贵的古玩花瓶而深感骄傲，以至于竟要把卧室漆成与花瓶同样的颜色。几名油漆匠努力想调出这个底色，但是谁也不能令那位古怪的老太婆满意。

最后，来了位油漆匠，自信能调出那种颜色。富婆对他做的活非常满意，油漆匠于是一举成名。

多年以后，他退休了，生意也交给了儿子。“爸爸，”儿子说：“有件事我想弄清楚，您是怎样使墙的颜色与花瓶配得那么完美的？”

“儿子，父亲回答说：我漆了花瓶。”

实战提升 Practising & Exercise

单词 & 词组

advantage [əd'vɑːntidʒ] *n.* 优势，有利条件，利益
disadvantage [ˌdisəd'vɑːntidʒ] *n.* 不利，不利条件，缺点，劣势
curse [kəːs] *n.* 诅咒，咒语，祸根，祸因
flavoring ['fleɪvərɪŋ] *n.* 调味品，调味料
hypocritical [ˌhipə'kritikəl] *adj.* 伪善的，伪善者的
deceiver [di'siːvə(r)] *n.* 欺人者，欺诈者
matron ['meitrən] *n.* 已婚老妇人
antique [æn'tiːk] *n.* 古物，古董
eccentric [ik'sentrik] *n.* 古怪，偏执的

知道不知道

match 常见表达

It is a match! 一言为定！就这样！
be no match for 比不上，不是……的对手
best match 最佳匹配；最佳配合
find [meet] one's match 遇到对手，棋逢对手
let beggars match with beggars. 龙配龙，凤配凤
make a match 作媒
make a match of it 结婚；促成一对
make a good match 找到好对象
meddle with your match 找一个和你势均力敌的人去欺负吧
play a match 比赛

I shall not come back
我将永远不回来了

Chaude and Cold

A **patron** in Montreal cafe turned on a tap in the washroom and got **scalded**. "This is an **outrage**," he complained. "The **faucet** marked C gave me boiling water."

"But, Monsieur, C stands for chaude – French for hot. You should know that if you live in Montreal."

"Wait a minute," roared the patron. "The other tap is also marked C."

"Of course," said the manager, "It stands for cold. After all, Montreal is a **bilingual** city."

热与冷

蒙特利尔自助餐厅的一位顾客拧开盥洗室的龙头，结果被水烫伤了。"这太可恶了，"他抱怨道，"标着 C 的龙头流出的是开水。"

"可是，先生，C 代表 Chaude – 法语里表示'热'的意思。如果您居住在蒙特利尔的话就得知道这一点。"

"等等，"那位顾客咆哮道，"另外一个龙头同样标的是 C。"

"当然，"经理说道："它代表冷。毕竟，蒙特利尔是个双语城市。"

★★★★★

Teacher：What great event happened in 1809？

Little Willy：Abraham Lincoln was born.

Teacher：Correct. And what great event happened in 1812？

Little Willy：Abraham Lincoln had his third birthday.

老师：1809 年发生了什么重大事件?

小威利：亚伯拉罕 – 林肯诞生。

老师：正确。那么 1812 年发生了什么重要事件呢?

小威利：亚伯拉罕 – 林肯过三周岁生日。

★★★★★

Crazy driver

There's a **senior** citizen driving on the highway. His wife calls him on his cell phone and in a worried voice says，"Herman，be careful! I just heard on the radio that there was a madman driving the wrong way on Route 280！"

Herman says，"I know，but there isn't just one，there are hundreds!"

疯狂的司机

一位高龄老人开着车在高速公路上驾车时，接到了妻子打来的电话。妻子焦急地告诉他说，"赫尔曼，小心！我刚从电台上听到报道说，在 280 号公路上有一个疯子正在逆行开车！"

赫尔曼说，"我知道，但不是一个，而是成百上千个！"

★★★★★

The umbrella

A gentleman staying in a hotel left his umbrella in the hall，but he had put on the handle a card on which was written: "This umbrella belongs to a gentleman who can lift up a hundred pounds. I shall be back in ten minutes." When he came back, he found, instead of his umbrella, another card on which was written, "This card belongs to a man who can run ten miles an hour. I shall not come back."

雨伞

一位住在旅馆的绅士把他的雨伞放在了大厅里，不过他在伞柄上系了一张卡片，上面写道，"此伞属于一位能举百磅的绅士。我将在十分钟内回来。"当他回来时，发现雨伞已经不翼而飞，取而代之的是另一张卡片，上面写着："此卡是一位一小时能跑十英里的人留下的，我再也不回来了。"

★★★★★

A girl just like mother

No matter which girl he brought home, the young man found disapproval from his mother. A friend gave him advice. "Find a girl just like your mother—then she's bound to like her."

So the young man searched and searched, and finally found the girl. He told his friendly adviser:

"Just like you said, I found a girl who looked, talked, dressed, and even cooked like mother. And just as you said, mother liked her."

"So," asked the friend, "what happened?"

"Nothing," said the young man. "My father hates her!"

和母亲一样的女孩

有位青年发现无论带哪一个女孩回家，总会遭到母亲的反对。一位朋友劝他说："找一个和你母亲一样的女孩——那她一定会喜欢她。”

于是这位青年人不停地找啊找，终于找到了这么个女孩。

他对这位朋友说：“正像你说的那样，我找到一个长相、谈吐、穿着打扮，甚至连烹饪都和我母亲一样的女孩。正像你说的那样，我母亲喜欢她。”

“那后来呢？”朋友问。

“没什么，”青年人说，“我父亲讨厌她！”

实战提升
Practising & Exercise

单词 & 词组

patron ['peitrən] *n.*（对某人，某种目标，艺术等）赞助人，资助人
scald [skɔːld] *n.* 烫伤，烫洗
outrage ['autreidʒ] *n.* 暴行，侮辱，愤怒
faucet ['fɔːsit] *n.* 龙头，旋塞，（连接管子的）插口
bilingual [bai'liŋgwəl] *adj.* 两种语言的
senior ['siːnjə] *adj.* 年长的，资格较老的，地位较高的，高级的

知道不知道

在法语系国家，一般通用的热水标志是用 C 代表冷水、H 代表热水；不过在法语系的国家，C 是 Chaud 的缩写，表示热水，而冷水却用 F，即 Froid 表示。

Time is money for both of us
时间对我们俩来说都是金钱

No cavities

A smiling boy arrived home from a dental visit, "Hey mom, the dentist says I have no **cavities**."

His mom stared at him wide-eyed and quite surprised, "It's impossible—you never **brush** your teeth after cleaning the chocolate box before you go to bed!"

Then the boy opened his mouth—he had not a tooth left!

我没有蛀牙

小男孩看完牙医，面带微笑地回到家："嘿，妈妈，牙医说，我一颗蛀牙也没有。"

妈妈惊讶地瞪大眼睛："不可能——你每回上床睡觉前都把巧克力吃完，而且从来不刷牙！"

这时，男孩张开了嘴巴——他的牙全被拔光了！

★★★★★

What is a traitor?

Young hopeful: "Father, what is a **traitor** in politics?"

Father (a veteran politician): "A traitor is a man who leaves our party and goes over to the other one."

Young hopeful: "Well then, what is a man who leaves his party and comes over to yours?"

Father: "A **convert**, my son."

什么叫叛徒?

有希望的青年人:"父亲,什么叫政治叛徒?"

父亲(一位老资格的政治家):"叛徒指的是离开我们党而加入到另一个党的人。"

有希望的青年人:"那么,离开他的党而加入到你们党的人又叫什么呢?"

父亲:"叫改变信仰者,我的儿子。"

★★★★★

A fat man and a skinny man were arguing about who was the more polite.

The skinny man said he was more polite because he always **tipped** his hat to ladies. But the fat man knew he was the more **courteous** because, whenever he got up and offered his seat, two ladies could sit down.

一个胖男人和一个瘦男人正在为谁更有礼貌而争吵。

瘦男人说他更礼貌,因为他总是向女士脱帽致意。但是胖男人说他更礼貌,因为无论何时他起身给女士让座,总是能让两位女士都坐下。

★★★★★

Time is money

As the taxi came to a **screeching halt** at a traffic light, I asked the driver, "Do you agree that 'Time is money'?"

"Well, it's a very common saying. Who will care so much about that?" the driver answered. "Look, the digits in the meter are still running when the car has stopped," I pointed at the meter.

"Oh, yes. You've got a point here. In this case, time is money for both of us." added the driver.

时间就是金钱

当出租车在遇到红灯急刹车时，我问司机："你同意'时间就是金钱'这种说法吗？"

"哦，这是一个俗语。在这个问题上，谁会在意那么多呢？"司机回答说。

"看，车都停了，里程表上的数字还在跑呢。"我指着里程表说。

"哦，是的。你说的挺有道理的。在这种情况下，时间对我们俩来说都是金钱。"司机补充说。

★★★★★

He loves chocolate chips

An old man was laying on his bed. He had only hours to live when he suddenly smelled chocolate chips. He loved chocolate chips more than anything else in the world. With his last bit of energy, he pulled himself out of bed, across the floor, and to the stairs. Then down the stairs and into the kitchen. There his wife was baking chocolate chips. As he reached for one, he got SMACKED across the back of his hand by the wooden spoon his wife was holding. "Leave them alone!" she said, "They're for the funeral!"

他爱吃巧克力曲奇

老头躺在床上，只能再活几个小时了。突然，他闻到了巧克力曲奇的味道，他最爱吃这种饼干了。因此他用最后一点力气，翻下床，爬到楼梯那，下楼到了厨房。他老伴正在做巧克力曲奇。他拿了一块正想吃，这时手背被老伴用木勺打了一下，“放下！”她说，“这是葬礼上用的！”

实战提升
Practising & Exercise

单词 & 词组

cavity ['kæviti] *n.* 洞，腔；窝
brush [brʌʃ] *n.* 刷子，毛刷，画笔
traitor ['treitə] *n.* 叛逆者，叛国者
convert [kən'vəːt] *n.* 皈依者
tip [tip] *n.* 顶，尖端
courteous ['kəːtjəs] *adj.* 有礼貌的，谦恭的
screech [skriːtʃ] *vt.* 尖声喊叫，尖叫声，急煞车声
halt [hɔːlt] *n.* 停止，暂停，中断

知道不知道

有关牙齿的词汇

a false tooth 假牙
canine tooth 犬牙，犬齿
incisor tooth 切牙，门齿
milk tooth 乳牙，乳齿
molar tooth 磨牙，臼齿
wisdom tooth 智牙，第三磨牙
periodontitis 牙周炎

Tell me when we get there
到那站时，请告诉我

Sleeping pills

Bob was having trouble getting to sleep at night. He went to see his doctor，who **prescribed** some extra-strong sleeping pills.

Sunday night Bob took the pills，slept well and was awake before he heard the alarm. He took his time getting to the office，**strolled** in and said to his boss：“I didn't have a bit of trouble getting up this morning.”

“That's fine，” roared the boss，“but where were you Monday and Tuesday？”

安眠药

鲍勃晚上总失眠。他去看医生，医生给他开了一些强力安眠药。

星期天晚上鲍勃吃了药，睡得很好，闹钟还没响他就醒了。他到了办公室，慢慢遛达进去，对老板说：“我今天早上起床很顺利。”

“很好！”老板吼道，“那你星期一和星期二到哪儿去了？”

★★★★★

Is he really ill ?

On a hot summer day an elderly gentleman **faints** in the street. A small crowd immediately gathers around him.

"Give the poor man a glass of brandy," advises a woman.

"Give him a heart massage," says someone else.

"No, just give him some brandy," insists the woman.

"Call an ambulance," yells another person.

"A brandy!"

The man suddenly sits up and **exclaims**. "Shut up, everybody, and do as the kind lady says!"

他是真的病了吗?

在一个炎热的夏天，一位上了年纪的男子昏倒在街头。人们立刻围了上去。

"给这个可怜的人一杯白兰地吧。"一位女士建议道。

"给他一点治心脏病的药。"另外一个人说。

"不，还是给他一些白兰地。"那位女士坚持说。

"叫辆救护车吧。"有人叫道。

"一杯白兰地！"

这时，那个人突然坐起来嚷道，"都闭嘴，就照那位好心的太太说得去做！"

★★★★★

Tell me when we get there

"Is this stop Bloomington ? " an old lady asked the busdriver.

"No, ma'am," the driver replied.

"Well, please tell me when we get there," she requested.

"I'll do that," promised the driver.

Later, the driver got careless and passed through Bloomington before he realized it. He apologized to the other passengers, turned around, and drove back. Then he said to the old lady: "This is the town where you wanted to get out." "Who wanted to get out?" she asked.

The driver said, "You did."

"No," she said, "my daughter told me that when I **pass through** this town, I should take my pills."

到那站时，请告诉我

有个老妇人问公共汽车司机："这站是布鲁明登吗？"

司机回答："不是的，太太。"

"那么，我们到那站时，请告诉我。"她说。

"我会的。"司机保证说。

后来，司机不小心忘了这件事，等他想起来的时候，汽车已经开过了布鲁明登。他向其他乘客道歉，掉转车头，开了回去。然后他对老妇人说："这就是你要下车的那个城镇。""谁要下车？"她问。

司机说："你啊。"

"不。"她说："我女儿跟我说，当我经过这个城镇时，我就该吃药了。"

★★★★★

Open-book exam

On the day of our final exam at my Community College in Santa Maria, Calif., we heard that the bookstore had changed its policy and would buy back our business-management textbooks. Before class, several of us dashed over to the store and sold our books. We were seated and waiting for the test when our professor announced that considering the difficulty of the final, it would be an open-book exam.

开卷考试

我在加利福尼亚的圣玛丽亚市一所社区大学读书时，有一次期末考试，我们听说书店在回购我们的工商管理课本。于是，我们几个赶忙跑到书店把书卖了，随后，我们坐在教室里等着考试。这时教授宣布：考虑到期末考试的难度，今天我们决定开卷考试。

实战提升
Practising & Exercise

单词 & 词组

prescribe [pris'kraib] *v.* 指示，规定，开药方

stroll [strəul] *v.* 闲逛，四处流浪

faint [feint] *adj.* 晕倒

exclaim [iks'kleim] *v.* 呼喊，惊叫

pass through 经过，痛快

知道不知道

open-book exam，开卷考试，闭卷考试就是 close-book，还有的考试允许考生带笔记，那就是 open-note。

可想而知，这几个卖了书的家伙恐怕要考砸了。I bombed the test. 我考砸了。bomb 的意思是轰炸，在口语中指的是“把什么东西搞砸了”。同样，要是约会时发挥失常，也可以说 I bombed on the date.

You can always tell which way the wind is blowing
你总能分清风是从哪边吹过来的

Good points and bad points

“This house,” said the real-estate salesman, “has both its good points and bad points. To show you I'm honest, I'm going to tell you about the disadvantage – there is a chemical plant one block south and a **slaughterhouse** one block north.”

“What are the advantages ? ” inquired the prospective buyer.

“The good thing about it,” said the agent, “is that you can always tell which way the wind is blowing.”

优缺点

“这幢房子,”房地产推销商说,“既有优点也有缺点。为了显示我的诚意,我会告诉你它的缺点。往南面一个街区是一家化工厂,往北面一个街区是一家屠宰场。”

“那么它的优点呢?”准备买房子的人问道。

代理商说道,“它的好处就是,你总能分清风是从哪边吹过来的。”

★★★★★

To buy a hat

A lady went to a hat shop to buy a hat. As she was very **fussy**, it took her a long time to pick out one. Already at the end of his patience the salesman was afraid that she might change her mind again so he tried to **flatter** her: "An excellent choice, madam. You look at least ten years younger with this hat on!"

To his **dismay**, the lady took off her hat at once and said: "I don't want a hat that makes me look ten years older as soon as I take it off. Show me some more hats!"

买帽子

一位女士到一家帽子店买帽子。她很挑剔，用了很长时间才选好一顶。已到忍耐极限的售货员害怕她再改变主意，赶紧恭维她："夫人，您的选择真明智。您戴上这顶帽子看上去起码年轻十岁！"

但令他沮丧的是，这位女士马上摘下了帽子说："我不想要一顶摘下来便立刻让我显得老十岁的帽子。多拿些帽子给我看看！"

★★★★★

Monkey business

A policeman took a monkey to his boss. The boss asked, "What kind of **monkey business** are you getting up to? He said," This monkey was wandering on the streets, not following any of the rules. I'm turning him in." The boss said, "Oh, my God! You're so dumb! If you catch a monkey, you have to take it to the zoo. Why bring it to me. Take it to the zoo!" So the policeman took the monkey out. Three or four days later, he was seen again, holding the monkey's hand. He took the monkey to the police car, opened the door, put it in, and was about to drive away. The boss saw this, ran out, and asked," Oh, my God! How come the monkey is still here？ I told you to take it to the zoo." The policeman replied，"Yes，sir. I've already taken him to the zoo. Today，I'm taking him to **see a movie**.

胡闹

有位警察带了只猴子给他上司看，他上司就说他："你搞什么鬼啊？"警察说："这猴子在大街上到处乱跑，不守规矩，我把它捉了回来。"上司说："天啊，你怎么那么笨？捉到猴子就把它带到动物园去嘛，带给我干吗？把它送到动物园去！"后来那警察就带了猴子出去了。三四天后，上司看见他拉着猴子的手，打开警车门让猴子坐进去，正准备开车出去。上司忙跑来说："天啊，为什么到现在还把猴子留在这儿，我不是叫你把它带到动物园去的吗？怎么还在这儿？"警察大哥说："是呀！我已经带它去了动物园，今天带它去看电影！"

★★★★★

Is that clock right

Dan was the **doorman** of a club in a big city. Everyday，thousands of people passed his door，and a lot of them stopped and asked him，"What's the time，please？"

After a few months，Dan said to himself，"I'm not going to answer all those stupid people any more. I'm going to buy a big clock and put it upon the wall here." Then he did so.

"Now people aren't going to stop and ask me the time，" he thought happily. But after that，a lot of people stopped，looked at the clock and then asked Dan，"Is that clock right？"

这钟准吗？

丹在一个大城市的某个俱乐部当守门人。每天都有数千人经过他的门口，而且许多人都会停下来问他："请问现在几点？"几个月后，丹想：“我不想再回答这些笨蛋提出的问题了，我要去买一只大钟，把它挂在这儿的墙上。”于是他买了一只钟，把它挂在了墙上。

“现在人们总不会再停下来问我时间了吧。”他高兴地想。可是打那以后，每天仍有许多人停下来，看看钟，然后问丹：“这钟准吗？”

实战提升 Practising & Exercise

单词 & 词组

slaughterhouse ['slɔːtəhaʊs] *n.* 屠宰场

fussy ['fʌsi] *adj.* 急躁，担忧的

flatter ['flætə] *vt.* 阿谀，奉承

dismay [dis'mei] *n.* 沮丧，惊慌

monkey business 胡闹，常指指不道德或不合法的行为；恶作剧

see a movie 看电影

doorman ['dɔːmən] *n.* 门卫，门童

知道不知道

迈克尔·杰克逊有首歌曲就叫 Monkey business。

Well，Lord have mercy
Well，Lord have mercy
This ain't no good for me
This ain't no good for me，baby
Well，Lord have mercy
Well，Lord have mercy
Ain't no good for me，baby
Tell me what's goin' down，baby

Every time I wanna say it，it is
Just too much for me...

When do people talk least ?
人们什么时候说话最少？

Best reward

A naval officer fell overboard. He was **rescued** by a deck hand. The officer asked how he could **reward** him.
“The best way, sir,” said the deck hand, “is to say nothing about it. If the other fellows knew I'd pulled you out, they'd **chuck** me in.”

最好的奖赏

一名海军军官从甲板上掉入海中。他被一名甲板水手救起。这位军官问如何才能酬谢他。
“长官，最好的办法，”这名水手说，“就是别声张这事。如果其他人知道我救了您，他们会把我扔下去的。”

★★★★★

Two pounds plums

Mother：I sent my little boy for two pounds of **plums** and you gave him a pound and a half.
Shopkeeper：My scales are all right，madam. Have you weighed your little boy？

两磅李子

母亲：我让小孩来买两磅李子，可你只给了他一磅半。

店主：太太，我们的秤准确无误。您秤过您的儿子了吗？

★★★★★

Things have been okay

A young couple were becoming **anxious** about their four-year-old son, who had not yet talked. They took him to specialists, but the doctors found nothing wrong with him. Then one morning at breakfast the boy suddenly **blurted**, "Mom, the toast is burned."

"You talked! You talked!" Shouted his mother. "I'm so happy! But **why has it taken this long**?"

"Well, up till now," Said the boy, "things have been okay."

一切都正常

一对年轻夫妇有个儿子，已经四岁了，还没有开口说话。他们对此深感焦虑，于是带他去找专家诊治，但医生们认为孩子一切正常。后来有一天吃早餐时，小男孩突然开口了："妈妈，面包烤焦了。

"你说话了！你说话了！"他母亲叫了起来。"我太高兴了！但为什么花了这么长的时间呢？"

"哦，在这之前，"那男孩说，"一切都正常啊。"

★★★★★

The bad news and the terrible news

Michael sat in his attorney's office. "Do you want the bad news first or the terrible news?" the lawyer asked.

"Give me the bad news first."

"Your wife found a picture worth a half-million dollars."

"That's the bad news ? " asked Michael **incredulously**. "I can't wait to hear the terrible news."

"The terrible news is that it's of you and your secretary."

坏消息和可怕的消息

迈克尔坐在律师的办公室里。"您想先知道坏消息还是可怕的消息?" 律师问。

"先告诉我坏消息吧。"

"您的妻子发现了一张价值 50 万美元的照片。"

"那是坏消息?" 迈克尔满腹怀疑,"快告诉我可怕的消息。"

"可怕的消息就是照片是关于您和秘书的。"

★★★★★

When do people talk least ?

Student A: When do people talk least ?

Student B: In February.

Student A: Why ?

Student B: Because February is the shortest month of the year.

★★★★★

人们什么时候说话最少?

学生甲:人们在什么时候说话最少?

学生乙:在二月。

学生甲:为什么呢?

学生乙:因为二月是一年中最短的一个月。

实战提升 Practising & Exercise

单词 & 词组

rescue ['reskjuː] *n.* 营救，救援

reward [ri'wɔːd] *vt.* 报酬，奖赏

chuck [tʃʌk] *n.*（随便或贸然地）扔，抛

plum [plʌm] *n.* 李子，梅子

anxious ['æŋkʃəs] *adj.* 焦急的，忧虑的

blurt [bləːt] *vt.* 突然说出，脱口而出

why has it taken this long，是 It takes sb. some time to do sth. 句式的变体。

incredulously [in'kredjuləsli] 不肯轻信地

知道不知道

有一首童谣是这样唱的：

30 days hath September，April，June，and November.
All the rest have 31
but February's the shortest one.
With 28 days most of the time
until Leap Year gives us 29.

Good news and bad news
好消息和坏消息

All I do is pay

"My family is just like a nation," Mr. Brown told his colleague. "My wife is the Minister of finance, my mother-in-law is the Minister of war, and my daughter is foreign secretary."

"Sounds interesting," his colleague replied. "And what is your position?"

"I'm the people. All I do is pay."

我要做的一切就是付钱

布朗先生告诉同事说:"我的家庭简直就像一个国家一样。我妻子是财政部长。我岳母是作战部长,我女儿是外交秘书。"

"听上去挺有意思的,"他的同事说,"那你的职务是什么呢?"

"我就是老百姓。我要做的一切就是付钱。"

★★★★★

Good news and bad news

"There's good news and bad news," the divorce lawyer told his client. "I could sure use some good news," sighed the client. "What's it?"

"Your wife isn't demanding that your future **inheritances** be included in the settlement."

"And the bad news ? "

"After the divorce，she's marrying your father."

好消息和坏消息

离婚诉讼律师告诉他的顾客"有好消息还有坏消息。"

"我能确信有些好消息，"客户叹气道："说说吧"。

"你的妻子没有对你未来继承的遗产提出要求。"

"那坏消息呢? "

"离婚后，她嫁给你父亲。"

★★★★★

I'll see to the rest

A guard was about to signal his train to start when he saw an **attractive** girl standing on the **platform** by an open door，talking to another pretty girl inside the **carriage**.

"Come on，Miss!" he shouted. "Shut the door，please!"

"Oh，I just want to kiss my sister goodbye," she called back.

"You just shut that door，please," called the guard，"and I'll see to the rest."

其余的事由我负责

一位列车员刚发出信号让火车启动，这时他看见一位很漂亮的姑娘站在站台上一节打开的车厢门旁边，跟车厢里另一位漂亮姑娘在说话。

"快点，小姐!"他喊道："请把门关上! "

"噢，我还没有和妹妹吻别呢。"她回答道。

"请把门关上，"列车员说："其余的事由我负责。"

实战提升 Practising & Exercise

单词 & 词组

inheritance [in'heritəns] *n.* 遗传，遗产
carriage ['kæridʒ] *n.* 马车，客车，运费
attractive [ə'træktiv] *adj.* 吸引人的，有魅力的
platform ['plætfɔːm] *n.*（车站）月台，讲台，讲坛

知道不知道

看到 I am the people 这句时，让人想起美国二十世纪的伟大作家、“芝加哥诗人”卡尔·桑德堡(Carl Sandburg)的那首诗:《我是人民、暴民》((I Am the People，the Mob)。他还有一句名言：三种东西不招自来：爱情，嫉妒和恐惧。(Three who come unbidden: love，jealousy，fear.)

A trip to disney
迪斯尼之旅

Absent-minded Professor

There were three professors at the railway station. They were deep in conversation. The train had just arrived, but they did not notice it. Then the guard shouted, "Take your seats, please!"

The professors heard the guard and rushed for the train. Two of them got on the train before it moved. The third one was left behind. It was Professor Egghead. He looked worried.

One of the professor's students was at the station. He tried to **comfort** the professor. "It wasn't really bad, sir," said the student. "Two out of three caught the train. That's quite good, you know." "I know," the professor said. "But it was my train. My friends only came to say goodbye."

心不在焉的教授

有三位教授在火车站里，他们正在聚精会神地谈话。火车进站了，他们都没有发觉。这时列车员喊道："请上车！"

教授们听到喊声后赶紧向火车跑去，两位教授登上了火车，另一位叫埃哈德的教授没能赶上。他看上去很着急。

这位教授的一个学生也在车站等车。他尽力安慰教授说："这还不是很糟，三个人有两个人上了火车。您要知道这已经不错了。"

教授说："我知道，可我是来赶火车的，那两位朋友是来为我送行的。"

★★★★★

A big head

"All the kids make fun of me," the boy cried to his mother. "They say I have a big head."

"Don't listen to them," his mother **consoled**. "You have a beautiful head. Now stop crying and go to the store for ten pounds of potatoes."

"Where's the shopping bag?"

"I haven't got one – use you hat."

大脑袋

"所有的小朋友都拿我取乐，"小男孩哭着跟妈妈说："他们说我长了一个大脑袋。"

"别听他们的，"他妈妈安慰说。"你的脑袋长得很漂亮。好了，别哭了，到店里买10磅土豆来。"

"兜子在哪呢？"

"我没有兜子——就用你的帽子吧。"

★★★★★

An advertisement for modern bicycle

Tom saw an advertisement in a newspaper for a beautiful modern bicycle which cost £50, so he went to the shop to have a look.

After examining the bicycle carefully, Tom turned to the shopkeeper and said, "There isn't a lamp on this bicycle, but there was one on the bicycle in your advertisement." "Yes, sir," answered the shopkeeper，“but the lamp isn't included in the price of the bicycle. It's an **extra**.”

“Not included in the price of bicycle?” Tom said angrily，“But that's not honest. If the lamp's in the advertisement，it should have been included in the price you gave there.”

“Well，sir，” answered the shopkeeper **calmly**，“there is also a girl on the bicycle in our advertisement，shall we **supply** one for you too？”

摩登自行车广告

汤姆在报纸上看到一辆很漂亮的摩登自行车的广告，标价50英镑，于是他到商店去看一看。

汤姆很仔细地看完那辆自行车后，转过身对店主说：“这辆自行车少了一盏灯，但在广告上的自行车是有的。”“是的，先生，”店主回答说，“但那盏灯不包括在自行车的价格里面，是另外收费的。”

“不包括在自行车价格里面？”汤姆很生气，“但这是不诚实的。如果灯在广告上，它就应该包括在你所标出的价格之内。”

“嗯，先生，”店主冷静地回答：“在我们的自行车广告上还有一个女孩，难道我们也要为您提供一个吗？”

实战提升 Practising & Exercise

单词 & 词组

absent-minded 心不在焉的，出神的
comfort ['kʌmfət] *n.* 安慰，舒适，安慰者
console [kən'səul] *vt.* 安慰，藉慰
extra ['ekstrə] *adv.* 特别地，非常，另外
supply [sə'plai] *n.* 补给，供给，供应品
calmly ['kɑːmli] *adv.* 平静地，安静地，冷静地

知道不知道

extra 用法详解

1. 用做形容词，表示“额外的”“另加的”，通常用作定语。
   We need extra money. 我们另外还需要一些钱。
2. 表示“另外收费的”，通常用作表语。
   Dinner costs 30 dollars, and wine is extra. 饭菜 30 美元，酒费在外。
3. 用做副词，表示“特别地”、“非常”，主要用来修饰形容词或副词。They worked extra hard. 他们工作特别努力。
4. 表示“额外地”“另加地”，主要用于收费方面，通常用来修饰动词（有时也放在名词后）。They charge extra for wine. 他们对酒另外收费。
5. 用做名词，意为“额外的钱或费用（即附加费）”“另收费项目”等，通常为可数名词。Breakfast is an extra at this hotel. 这家旅馆早餐要另外收费。
6. 有时表示“（演群众角色的）临时演员”“（报纸的）号外”等。

Good-bye, money
再见，钞票

A Trip to Disney

On a trip to Disney World in Florida, my husband and I and our two children devoted ourselves wholeheartedly to the wonders of this attraction. After three **exhausting** days, we **headed for** home.

As we drove away, our son waved and said, "Good-bye, Mickey."

Our daughter waved and said, "Good-by, Minnie."

My husband waved, rather weakly, and said, "Good-bye, Money."

迪斯尼之旅

弗罗里达州的迪斯尼乐园是一个迷人的地方。一次我和丈夫以及两个孩子前往旅游，我们全身心地沉醉在它的各种奇观之中。精疲力竭地玩了三天之后，我们要回家了。

当我们驱车离开时，儿子挥手说："再见，美奇。"

女儿挥着手说，"再见，美妮。"

丈夫也有气无力地挥了挥手，说道："再见，钞票。"

★★★★★

The top nine most popular reasons for not doing homework:

1. My computer **crashed** and I lost it.
2. I finished my homework but then I deleted it by accident.
3. I could not print it out.
4. My internet was down so I could not do any research.
5. I lost my **laptop**.
6. My dad's computer was hacked by the Russians and they stole my homework.
7. A burglar stole my printed-out homework along with the computer.
8. The PC exploded when our dog went to the toilet on it.
9. I accidentally tipped a bottle of **cider** over the computer and it broke.

九个不做作业最流行的借口：

1. 电脑死机了，我做的作业（因没有保存）丢失了。
2. 虽然我已经完成了作业，但后来不小心把它删除了。
3. 打印机坏了，作业打不出来。
4. 网断了，我没法上网查资料。
5. 我的笔记本电脑丢了。
6. 我爸爸的电脑被俄罗斯黑客入侵，他们偷走了我的作业。
7. 有个贼把我打印好的作业连同电脑一齐偷走了。
8. 我家的狗狗把电脑当厕所，结果把电脑弄炸了。
9. 我不小心把一杯苹果汁洒在电脑上，电脑就坏了。

实战提升
Practising & Exercise

单词 & 词组

exhausting [ig'zɔːstiŋ] *adj.* 使用尽的，令人疲乏不堪的
head for 出发，动身，前往
crash [kræʃ] *n.* 碰撞，坠落
laptop ['læptap] *n.* 便携式电脑
cider ['saidə] *n.* 苹果酒

知道不知道

苹果酒为低度酒，含有较丰富的营养，适量饮用可舒筋活络，增进身体健康。发酵苹果汁在美国又叫硬苹果汁（hard cider），在英国、法国、澳在利亚等国叫苹果酒。根据加工方法和产品的特点可将苹果酒分为发酵苹果酒、气酒和露酒等几种。发酵苹果酒是用苹果汁发酵菌发酵酿制而成。气酒是含二氧化碳的苹果酒，又称发泡酒。露酒一般是用食用酒精浸泡果实或与果汁配制而成。

A new employee
新员工

A smart housewife

A smart housewife was told that there was a kind of stove which would only consume half of the coal she was burning.

She was very excited, and said: “That'll be **terrific**! Since one stove can save half of the coal, if I buy two, no coal will be needed.”

精明的家庭主妇

一位精明的家庭主妇听说有一种炉子用起来可以比她现在用的炉子省一半的煤。

她听了大为兴奋，说：“太好了！一个炉子可以省一半的煤，那么如果我买两个炉子的话，不就可以把煤全都省下来了吗？”

★★★★★

A heavy sleeper

The **preacher** was **vexed** because a certain member of his **congregation** always fell asleep during the **sermon**.

As the man was snoring in the front row one Sunday, the preacher determined he would teach him not to sleep during the sermon. So, in a whisper, he asked the congregation. "All who want to go to heaven, please rise." Everyone got up except the snorer. After whispering "Be seated", the minister shouted at the top of his voiced, "All those who want to be with the devil, please rise."

Awaking with a start, the sleepy-head jumped to his feet and saw the preacher standing tall and angry in the **pulpit**, "Well, sir," he said, "I don't know what we're **voting on**, but it looks like you and me are the only ones for it."

瞌睡者

牧师非常生气，因为总有一个人在他布道时打瞌睡。

一个星期天，正当坐在前排的那个人又在瞌睡时，牧师决定要好好教育他一下，让他不要再在布道时睡觉。于是他低声对信徒们说："想去天堂的人，都请站起来吧。"所有的人都站了起来——当然，除了那个打瞌睡的人。在低声说过请坐后，牧师高声喊道："想下地狱的人请站起来！"

打瞌睡的人被这突然的喊叫声惊醒了，他站了起来。看到牧师高站在教坛上，正生气地看着他。这个人说道："噢，先生，我不知道我们在选什么，但看上去只有你和我是候选人。"

★★★★★

A new employee

Several weeks after a young man had been hired, he was called into the personnel director's office.

"What is the meaning of this?" the director asked. "When you appiied for the job, you told us you had five years'experience. Now we discover this is the first job you ever held."

"Well," the young man said, "in your advertisement you said you wanted somebody with **imagination**."

新员工

一个年轻人在被雇用几个星期后，被叫到人事经理的办公室。

“这是什么意思？”经理问，“当你申请这份工作时，你告诉我们有五年工作经验，现在我们发现这其实是你的第一份工作。”

“嗯，”年轻人回答，“你们的广告上说需要找一个有想象力的人嘛。”

★★★★★

Guns buried in the garden

An old man lived alone in Northern Ireland. His only son was in prison. The old man wanted to plant some potatoes in his garden but he didn't know anyone who would help him **plow up** the garden.

He wrote to his son about it, and received this reply, "For HEAVENS SAKE, don't dig up that garden, that's where I buried the GUNS!"

At 4 AM the next morning, a dozen British soldiers showed up and dug up the entire garden, but didn't find any guns.

Confused, the man wrote to his son telling him what happened and asking him what to do next.

His son's reply was: "Just plant your potatoes."

埋在花园里的枪

一个老人独居在北爱尔兰，他的独生子正在坐牢。老人想在花园里种些土豆，但不知道谁可以帮忙把泥土翻松。他写信想儿子提及此事，儿子回信说道："看在上帝的面上，千万不要翻松花园的泥土，我把枪埋在那儿了。"

第二天凌晨4点，一队英国士兵出现在老人家中，在花园把土地翻遍，但并没有找到任何枪支。"

老人写信告诉儿子这件奇怪的事情，问到底发生了什么事情，下一步应该怎么做。

儿子回信道："你只管种土豆好了。"

实战提升 Practising & Exercise

单词 & 词组

terrific [tə'rifik] *adj.* 令人恐怖的，极好的
preacher ['priːtʃə(r)] *n.* 传教士；讲道
vex [veks] *vt.* 使烦恼，恼怒
congregation [ˌkɔngri'geiʃən] *n.* 集合，集会，[宗] 圣会
sermon ['səːmən] *n.* 训诫，说教，布道
pulpit ['pulpit] *n.*（教堂的）讲道坛
vote on 表决
imagination [iˌmædʒi'neiʃən] *n.* 想象，空想，想象的事物
plow up 犁出，犁掉；深翻，深耕
confuse 搞乱，使糊涂

知道不知道

"布道"是圣经中的要道，因为福音是圣经基本的信息。主耶稣的大使命，可指为布道的大宪章。布道是使万民作主的门徒，这大使命记载在马太福音廿八章十八至廿节，可分为三大要项，都以分词 (participle) 来说明："去，使万民作门徒"、"给他们施洗"、"教训他们"。

Cannonical Murphy's laws of combat
墨菲定律（战场版）

1. Friendly fire – isn't.
   友军火力一点儿都不友好。（美军术语 Friendly fire 是指“被自己人误伤”）

2. Recoilless rifles – aren't.
   无坐力炮的后坐力大着呢。

3. Suppressive fires – won't.
   压制火力啥也压制不了。

4. You are not Superman；Marines and fighter pilots take note.
   你不是超人，陆战队员和战斗机飞行员特别要紧记这一条。

5. A sucking chest wound is Nature's way of telling you to slow down.
   胸口被打个大洞，你就自然而然会停下来。（sucking 是正在飙血的意思）

6. If it's stupid but it works，it isn't stupid.
   如果一个蠢方法有用，那它就不是一个蠢方法。

7. Try to look unimportant；the enemy may be low on ammo and not want to waste a bullet on you.
装成无关紧要的人，敌人可能子弹不多，不想浪费在你身上。

8. If at first you don't succeed，call in an air strike.
如果你的攻击没成功，马上呼叫空袭支援吧。

9. If you are forward of your position，your artillery will fall short.
每当你开始进攻时，炮兵也会越打越近。

10. Never share a foxhole with anyone braver than yourself.
永远别跟比你勇敢的战友呆在同一个散兵坑里。

11. Never go to bed with anyone crazier than yourself.
永远别跟比你疯狂的人一起睡觉。

12. Never forget that your weapon was made by the lowest **bidder**.
永远别忘了你手上的武器是由出价最低的承包商中标制造的。

13. If your attack is going really well，it's an **ambush**.
如果你的攻击进行得很顺利，那一定是你中了圈套。

14. The enemy **diversion** you're ignoring is their main attack.
那支你以为是佯动的敌兵其实是主攻部队。

15. The enemy invariably attacks on two occasions: a. When they're ready. b. When you're not.
敌人总会在以下两种情况发生时展开攻击：1) 他们准备好的时候；2) 你没准备好的时候。

16. No OPLAN ever survives initial contact.
任何作战计划在接敌之后都会变成废纸。

17. There is no such thing as a perfect plan.
完美的计划是不存在的。

18. Five second **fuses** always burn three seconds.
手榴弹的五秒引信总会在三秒内烧完。

19. There is no such thing as an atheist in a foxhole.
散兵坑里不存在无神论者。

20. A retreating enemy is probably just falling back and regrouping.
逃跑的敌军大概只是打算先撤退后反击。

21. The important things are always simple；the simple are always hard.
重要的事情总是简单的；简单的事情总是难以做到的。

22. The easy way is always **mined**.
好走的路总已被布上地雷。

23. Teamwork is essential；it gives the enemy other people to shoot at.
集体行动非常必要；起码敌人有其他目标可以射击了。

24. Don't look **conspicuous**；it draws fire. For this reason，it is not at all uncommon for aircraft carriers to be known as bomb magnets.
不要太显眼，因为那会吸引敌方火力。因此，航空母舰被称作"炸弹磁铁"就不奇怪了。

25. Never draw fire；it irritates everyone around you.

不要吸引敌人火力；这会使你身边所有的人都恨你。

26. If you are short of everything but the enemy，you are in the **combat** zone.

如果你除了敌人什么都缺，那你一定在交战区了。

27. When you have secured the area，make sure the enemy knows it too.

你攻占一个地区后，确保敌人也知道。

28. Incoming fire has the right of way.

飞来的子弹有优先通行权。（不要把身体挡在子弹的去路上）

29. No combat ready unit has ever passed inspection.

从来没有一支完成战备的单位能通过检阅。

30. No inspection ready unit has ever passed combat.

从来没有一支准备好检阅的部队能活过战斗。

31. If the enemy is within range，so are you.

如果敌人进入你的射程内，别忘了你也在进入了他的射程内。

32. The only thing more accurate than incoming enemy fire is incoming friendly fire.

唯一比敌军炮火还准确是友军火力。

33. Things that must be together to work can never be shipped together.

必须要装配在一起才能发挥效力的武器装备不能一起运送。

34. Things that must work together，can't be carried to the field that way.
必须要装配在一起才能发挥效力的武器不能被一起运到战场。

35. Radios will fail as soon as you need fire support
无线电总是在你急需火力支援时失灵。

36. Radar tends to fail at night and in bad weather，and especially during both).
雷达总是在晚上和坏天气时失灵，尤其是在两者都发生的时候。

37. Anything you do can get you killed，including nothing.
你所做的任何事都可能送命，就算你什么都不做也一样。

38. Make it too tough for the enemy to get in，and you won't be able to get out.
当你防守严密到敌人攻不进来时，那往往你自己也打出不去。

39. **Tracers** work both ways.
曳光弹是双刃剑。(你更容易打中敌人，敌人也更容易找到你的位置)

40. If you take more than your fair share of objectives，you will get more than your fair share of objectives to take.
如果你在行动中完成了额外的任务，那么你总会被赋予这些额外的任务。

41. When both sides are convinced they're about to lose，they're both right.
当两军都觉得自己快输时，那他们可能都是对的。

42. Professional soldiers are **predictable**; the world is full of dangerous **amateurs**.

专业士兵的行为是可预测的；但世上却充满了菜鸟。

43. Military Intelligence is a contradiction.

“军事情报”一词中的军事和情报是矛盾的。(intelligence 一词多义，同时也指“智慧”，这个双关语是讽刺战场上往往缺乏有头脑的行为)

44. Fortify your front；you'll get your rear shot up.

脑袋和屁股从来不可兼顾。

45. Weather ain't neutral.

天气不是中立的。(气像状况总是对你不利)

46. If you can't remember，the Claymore is pointed towards you.

如果你记不起来自己亲手布置的定向雷的指向，那这定向雷一定是朝向你的。

47. Air defense motto: shoot 'em down；sort 'em out on the ground.

防空座右铭：先把飞机打下来，再在地上区分敌友。

48. Flies high，it dies；low and slow，it'll go.

飞得高，死得快；飞得又低又慢，就能完成目标。

49. The Cavalry doesn't always come to the rescue.

不能把希望寄托在救兵身上。(言下之意是要靠自己，不要老想着会有人来救你。Cavalry 在美军俚语里就是“救兵”的意思，请想像一下当你处身美国西部开拓时期在野外被一大群印弟安人包围的情景)

50. Napalm is an area support weapon.

凝固汽油弹一炸一大片。（别扔得太近）

51. Mines are equal opportunity weapons.

地雷是机会均等的武器。

52. B–52s are the ultimate close support weapon.

B52 是终极近距支援武器。

53. Sniper's motto: reach out and touch someone.

狙击手座右铭：出去，干掉点儿人。

54. Killing for peace is like screwing for virginity.

“为了和平而杀戮”，就像是说为了贞洁而玩叉叉（screwing 这个“上螺线”的动作是形容词啦）一样。

55. The one item you need is always in short supply.

你需要的物品总是很缺乏。

56. Interchangeable parts aren't.

通用部件总是不通用。

57. It's not the one with your name on it；it's the one addressed “to whom it may concern” you've got to think about.

专门给你的指示一点也不重要；那些“致有关人士”的指示才是你必须重视的。

58. When in doubt，empty your magazine.

有怀疑的时候，先打空你的弹匣再说。

59. The side with the simplest uniforms wins.
制服最简单的一方总会获胜。

60. Combat will occur on the ground between two adjoining maps.
战斗总会在两张地图交汇的地方展开。（你总也拿不到战区的地图）

61. If the Platoon Sergeant can see you，so can the enemy.
如果副排长能看得见你，那敌人也能。

62. Never stand when you can sit，never sit when you can lie down，never stay awake when you can sleep.
能坐着的时候绝不要站着，能躺着的时候绝不要坐着，能睡着的时候绝不要醒着。

63. The most dangerous thing in the world is a Second Lieutenant with a map and a compass.
世上最可怕的东西是一个有地图和指南针的少尉。（他们擅长纸上谈兵）

64. Exceptions prove the rule，and destroy the battle plan.
例外才是战斗法则的最佳证明，作战计划滚一边去。

65. Everything always works in your HQ，everything always fails in the Colonel's HQ.
所有东西都在你的总部有效，在上校的总部失效。

66. The enemy never watches until you make a mistake.
敌人从来都不会察觉，除非你犯了错误。

67. One enemy soldier is never enough，but two is entirely too many.

一个敌人士兵永远不够，两个就太多了。

68. A clean (and dry) set of BDU's is a magnet for mud and rain.

清洁干净的作战服总是吸引泥和雨。

69. The worse the weather，the more you are required to be out in it.

天气越差，你被派遣出去的机会就越多。

70. Whenever you have plenty of **ammo**，you never miss. Whenever you are low on ammo，you can't hit the broad side of a barn.

你有足够弹药的时候，你百发百中。你缺弹药的时候，连谷仓那么大的东西都打不中。

71. The more a weapon costs，the farther you will have to send it away to be repaired.

武器越贵，修理的时候就要送的越远。

72. The complexity of a weapon is inversely proportional to the IQ of the weapon's operator.

武器的复杂程度和操作者的智商成反比。

73. Field experience is something you don't get until just after you need it.

“战场经验”这东西，只有在某次很需要它的行动之后你才能获得。

74. No matter which way you have to march，its always uphill.

不管你从哪条路线行军，都是上坡路。

75. If enough data is collected，a board of inquiry can prove anything.

如果收集到了足够的资料，调查委员会什么事都可以证明。(委员会胡说八道)

76. For every action，there is an equal and opposite criticism. (in boot camp)

在新兵训练营，对每一个行动都有赞成与反对两种评判。

77. Air strikes always overshoot the target，**artillery** always falls short.

空袭总是打得过远，炮火总是打得太近。

78. When reviewing the radio frequencies that you just wrote down，the most important ones are always illegible.

当你查看你写下的无线电频率的时候，最重要的总是无法辨认。

79. Those who hesitate under fire usually do not end up KIA，WIA or MIA.

交火中踌躇不前的家伙，通常不会有阵亡、重伤或失踪的下场。

80. The tough part about being an officer is that the troops don't know what they want，but they know for certain what they don't want.

作为军官最辛苦的一点是：士兵不知道他们想要什么，只知道他们不想要什么。

81. To steal information from a person is called plagiarism. To steal information from the enemy is called gathering intelligence.
从一个人那里偷取信息叫剽窃，从敌人那里偷取信息叫搜集情报。

82. The weapon that usually jams when you need it the most is the M60.
在你最需要它的时候总是卡壳的武器是 M60 机枪。

83. The perfect officer for the job will transfer in the day after that billet is filled by someone else.
最适合某个工作的军官总是在这个职位已经被别人占据后一天调来。

85. The newest and least experienced soldier will usually win the Medal of Honor.
最新最没经验的士兵最可能获得荣誉奖章。(意思是“挂掉的人就会获得美国最高级勋章”)

86. A Purple Heart just proves that were you smart enough to think of a plan，stupid enough to try it，and lucky enough to survive.
紫心勋章(美国授予受伤士兵的勋章)证明你聪明到可以想出一个计划，愚蠢到尝试这个计划，并且幸运到活了下来。

87. Murphy was a grunt.
墨菲是个大头兵。(就是因为墨菲老是做错事，所以才叫墨菲法则)

88. Beer Math –2 beers times 37 men equals 49 cases.
啤酒数计算法：三十七人，每人两瓶，共要四十九箱。

89. Body count Math -- 3 guerrillas plus 1 probable plus 2 pigs equals 37 enemies killed in action.
歼敌数计算法：三名游击队员加一个可能再加两只猪，本次战斗共毙敌三十七人。

90. The bursting radius of a hand **grenade** is always one foot greater than your jumping range.
手榴弹的杀伤半径总是比你能扑出的距离多一英尺。

91. All–weather close air support doesn't work in bad weather.
全天候近距空中支援在坏天气里不管用。

92. The combat worth of a unit is inversely proportional to the smartness of its outfit and appearance.
一支部队的作战能力与它外表的好看程度成反比。

93. The crucial round is a dud.
至关重要的炮弹总是哑弹。

95. There is no such place as a convenient **foxhole**.
需要散兵坑时，它们总是太远。（注：convenient 在这里是指地理上的便利，就好像所谓的便利店一样，所以不能作“舒适”解）

97. If your positions are firmly set and you are prepared to take the enemy assault on，he will bypass you.
如果你的阵地有很好的工事而且你也准备好应付敌人的攻击，敌人会绕过你。

98. If your ambush is properly set，the enemy won't walk into it.

如果你准备好了一次伏击，敌人不会进入你的伏击圈。

99. If your flank march is going well，the enemy expects you to outflank him.

如果你的侧翼迂回进行的很顺利，是因为敌人正期待着你从侧翼接近他们。

100. Density of fire increases proportionally to the curiousness of the target.

你越是感到好奇的目标就越危险。

101. Odd objects attract fire—never lurk behind one.

奇怪的物体吸引炮火——不要躲在这种东西后面。

103. The self-importance of a superior is inversely proportional to his position in the hierarchy (as is his deviousness and mischievousness).

长官的自大程度与他的官职成反比（还有他的不值得信任程度和有害程度）。

104. There is always a way，and it usually doesn't work.

任何事情都有一个解决方法，尽管通常是不管用的。

105. Success occurs when no one is looking，failure occurs when the General is watching.

没人关注的行动通常是成功的；被高级长官关注的行动通常是失败的。

106. The enemy never monitors your radio frequency until you broadcast on an unsecured channel.

在你使用不安全的频道发布之前，敌人都不会监听你的无线电频率。

107. Whenever you drop your equipment in a fire-fight，your ammo and grenades always fall the farthest away，and your canteen always lands at your feet.
如果你战斗中掉了装备，你的子弹和手榴弹一定离你最远，而水壶总是掉在你的脚边。

108. As soon as you are served hot chow in the field，it rains.
战场上，你只要搞到热东西吃，就总是要下雨的。

109. Never tell the Platoon Sergeant you have nothing to do.
不要告诉副排长你无事可做。

111. Walking point = sniper bait.
去带路 = 去当狙击手的诱饵。

112. Your bivouac for the night is the spot where you got tired of marching that day.
你夜间的宿营地是你白天行军累了的地方。

113. If only one solution can be found for a field problem，then it is usually a stupid solution.
如果一个战场上的问题只有一种解决方案，这一定是个愚蠢的方案。

115. What gets you promoted from one rank gets you killed in the next rank.
你在低军衔时能让你升官的行为会在新军衔时杀死你。

116. If orders can be misunderstood they will be.

如果命令可能被误解，那它一定会被误解。

117. Odd objects attract fire. You are odd.

奇怪的东西吸引炮火。你就是奇怪的。

118. Your mortar barrage will put exactly one round on the intended target. That round will be a dud.

迫击炮弹幕只有一发能命中目标，这一发是哑弹。

119. Mine fields are not neutral.

雷场不是中立的。

120. The weight of your equipment is proportional to the time you have been carrying it.

装备的重量与你需要扛着它的时间成正比。

122. If you need an officer in a hurry take a nap.

军官总是在你犯错误时出现。

123. The effective killing radius is greater than the average soldier can throw it.

投掷武器的杀伤半径总比一般士兵能扔的距离大。

128. When you have sufficient ammo the enemy takes 2 weeks to attack. When you are low on ammo the enemy attacks that night.

你弹药充足的时候，敌人两个礼拜也不进攻；你缺弹药的时候，敌人马上就进攻。

129. The quartermaster has only two sizes，too large and too small.

军需官那里的东西只有两个尺码：太大的和太小的。

130. The only time suppressive fire works is when it is used on abandoned positions.

压制火力唯一管用的时候是用来对付废弃的阵地的时候。

131. When a front line soldier overhears two General Staff officers conferring，he has fallen back too far.

如果一个前线士兵无意中听到两个参谋在讨论，那他一定是站得太靠后了。（参谋都是胆小鬼）

132. Don't ever be the first，don't ever be the last，and don't ever volunteer to do anything.

不要做第一个，也不要做倒数第一个，更不要志愿干什么事。

133. If at first you don't succeed，then bomb disposal probably isn't for you.

如果你进攻失败，轰炸计划可不是帮你忙的。

134. Any ship can be a minesweeper...once.

所有船只都可以当扫雷艇……一次性的。

135. Whenever you lose contact with the enemy，look behind you.

如果你失去了敌人的踪迹，转头看看。

136. If you find yourself in front of your platoon they know something you don't.

在战场上，如果你的位置过于靠前，那么你一定要注意是否忽视了某些潜在的危险。

137. The seriousness of a wound (in a firefight) is inversely proportional to the distance to any form of cover.
交火后，受伤的严重程度与到掩体的距离成反比。

138. The more stupid the leader is，the more important missions he is ordered to carry out.
指挥官越蠢，他被命令执行的任务越重要。

139. When the pin is pulled，Mr. Grenade is not your friend.
拔下保险销后，手榴弹先生就不再是你的朋友了。

140. All or any of the above combined.
以上法则的任意组合。

实战提升 Practising & Exercise

单词 & 词组

conspicuous [kən'spikjuəs] *adj.* 显著的

foxhole ['faks,hol] *n.* 散兵坑

bidder ['bidə] *n.* 出价人，投标人

ambush ['æmbuʃ] *n.* 埋伏，伏兵

grenade [gri'neid] *n.* 手榴弹

fuse [fju:z] *n.* 保险丝，熔丝

ammo ['æməu] *n.* < 俚 > 弹药，军火

artillery [ɑ:'tiləri] *n.* 炮的总称，炮兵的总称

diversion [dai'və:ʃən] *n.* 转移，转换

mine [main] *n.* 矿，矿山

combat ['kɔmbət] *n.* 战斗，格斗

desperately ['dɛspəritli] *adv.* 拼命地，失望地

tracer ['treisə] *n.* 追踪者，描图者

predictable [pri'diktəb(ə)l] *adj.* 可预言的

amateur ['æmətə(:)] *n.* 业余爱好者，业余艺术家

知道不知道

墨菲定律（Murphy's Law）是西方世界常用的俚语。墨菲定律主要内容是：事情如果有变坏的可能，不管这种可能性有多小，它总会发生。比如你衣袋里有两把钥匙，一把是你房间的，一把是汽车的，如果你现在想拿出车钥匙，会发生什么？是的，你往往是拿出了房间钥匙。“墨菲定律”、“派金森定理”和“彼得原理”并称为二十世纪西方文化中最杰出的三大发现。墨菲定律并不是一种强调人为错误的概率性定律，而是阐述了一种偶然中的必然性。

New baby
新生儿

Have you ceased beating your wife

This story is told of a browbeating counsel，who habitually endeavored to terrorize his opponent's witnesses.

One witness rather tended to preface his replies with lengthy explanations.

“I want ‘yes’ or ‘no,’” thundered counsel. “There is no need for you to argue the point！”

“But there are some questions which cannot be answered by ‘yes’ or ‘no,’” mildly responded the witness.

“There are not！” snapped the lawyer.

“Oh,” said the witness，“answer this then：“Have you ceased beating your wife？”

你停止打你妻子了吗?

这个故事讲的是一个咄咄逼人的辩护律师，他惯于设法恐吓对方的证人。

有一个证人习惯于在回答问题之前先做番冗长的解释。

“我要你回答‘是’或者‘不是’，”辩护律师怒喝道：“你没有必要就这个问题进行辩论。”

“可是有些问题无法用‘是’或者‘不是’来回答。”这位证人温和地回敬他。

“不存在这样的问题！”律师愚蠢地厉声说。
“噢，”证人说：“那么回答这个问题：你停止打你妻子了吗？”
★★★★★

The new baby

Mr. and Mrs. Taylor had a seven-year-old boy named Pat. Now Mrs. Taylor was expecting another child.

Pat had seen babies in other people's houses and had not liked them very much, so he was not **delighted** about the news that there was soon going to be one in his house too.

One evening Mr. and Mrs. Taylor were making plans for the baby's arrival. "This house won't be big enough for us all when the baby comes," said Mr. Taylor.

Pat came into the room just then and said, "What are you talking about ?" "We were saying that we'll have to move to another house now, because the new baby's coming," his mother answered.

"It's no use," said Pat **hopelessly**, "He'll follow us there."

新生儿

泰勒夫妇有一个七岁的男孩，名叫帕特。现在泰勒太太正怀着第二胎。

帕特在别人家看见过婴儿，他不太喜欢他们，所以他对自己家里也将有一个婴儿的消息感到不满。

一天晚上，泰勒夫妇正在为这个婴儿的降生计划做安排。泰勒先生说：“有了婴儿，我们的房子就太小，不够住了。”

帕特恰好在这个时候走进屋，他问：“你们在说什么？”他的母亲回答说：“我们在说我们得搬家，因为婴儿就要诞生了。”

“搬了房子也不够用，”帕特绝望地说，“他也会跟我们到那儿去的。”
★★★★★

Midway tactics

Three competing store owners rented **adjoining** shops in a mall. Observers waited for **mayhem** to **ensue**.

The retailer on the right put up huge signs saying, "Gigantic Sale!" and "Super Bargains!"

The store on the left raised bigger signs **proclaiming**, "Prices **Slashed**!" and "Fantastic **Discounts**!"

The owner in the middle then prepared a large sign that simply stated, "**ENTRANCE**".

中间战术

三个互相抢生意的商店老板在一个购物中心里租用了毗邻的店铺。旁观者等着瞧好戏。

右边的零售商挂起了巨大的招牌，上书："大减价！""特便宜！"

左边的商店挂出了更大的招牌，声称："大削价！""超折扣！"

中间的商人随后准备了一个大招牌，上面只简单地写着："入口处"。

★★★★★

"Excuse me, but the seat you've taken is mine."

"Yours? Can you prove it?"

"Yes, I put a cup of ice cream on it."

"请原谅，你占了我的位置。"

"你的位置？你能证明这点吗？"

"能，我在座位上放了杯冰激凌。"

实战提升 Practising & Exercise

单词 & 词组

delight [di'lait] *n.* 快乐，高兴，喜悦
hopelessly ['hoplisli] *adv.* 无望地，绝望地
adjoin [ə'dʒɔin] *v.* 邻接，毗连
mayhem ['meihem] *n.* 伤害罪之一种，故意的伤害罪
ensue [in'sjuː] *vi.* 跟着发生，继起
proclaim [prə'kleim] *vt.* 宣布，声明，显示，显露
slash [slæʃ] *v.* 猛砍，鞭打，砍伤
discount ['diskaunt] *n.* 折扣
entrance ['entrəns] *n.* 入口，门口，进入

知道不知道

律师的说法有多少种

lawyer 也是 attorney，solicitor，barrister，counselor (or counselor)，advocate 等的通称。

attorney 代理人、(小) 律师、讼师、辩护士。用法：an attorney represents his client - 律师代表当事人，美式英语用法。早期在英国指检察总长；在美国则为司法部长。

solicitor 英国 – 初级律师 ；美国 – 法务官

barrister 英国 – 大律师、辩护士

counsellor (or counselor) 英国 – 大律师、私人顾问；爱尔兰、美国 – 辩护士

advocate 辩护士、代言人、拥护者、提倡者

The Bar (法庭中的) 围栏；律师职、律师界

Violin lessons
小提琴课

Violin lessons

"Daddy, can I learn to play the violin?" young Sarah asked her father. She was always asking for things and her father was not very pleased.

"You cost me a lot of money, Sarah," he said. "First you wanted to learn horse riding, then dancing, then swimming. Now it's the violin."

"I'll play every day, Daddy." Sarah said. "I'll try very hard."

"All right," her father said. "This is what I'll do. I'll pay for you to have lessons for six weeks. At the end of six weeks you must play something for me. If you play well, you can have more lessons. If you play badly, I will stop the lessons."

"OK. Daddy," Sarah said. "That is fair."

He soon found a good violin teacher and Sarah began her lessons. The teacher was very expensive, but her father **kept his promise**.

The six weeks passed quickly. The time came for Sarah to play for her father.

She went to the living room and said, "I'm ready to play for you, Daddy."

"Fine, Sarah," her father said. "Begin."
She began to play. She played very badly. She made a terrible noise.
Her father had one of his friends with him, and the friend put his hands over his ears.
When Sarah finished, her father said, "**Well done**, Sarah. You can have more lessons."
Sarah ran happily out of the room. Her father's friend turned to him. "You've spent a lot of money, but she still plays very badly." he said.
"Well, that's true," her father said. "But since she started learning the violin I've been able to buy five apartments in this building very cheaply. In another six weeks I'll own the whole building!"

小提琴课

"爸爸，我能学拉小提琴吗？"小莎拉问她的父亲。她总是提出各种要求，因此她爸爸很不高兴。
"你花了我很多钱，莎拉，"他说，"开始你想学骑马，接着想学跳舞，然后是游泳。现在又想学拉小提琴。"
"我会每天都拉的，爸爸，"莎拉说，"我会认真练琴的。"
"好吧，"她爸爸说。"下面是我要做的：我会为你付六个星期的小提琴课的学费，六个星期后你必须拉首曲子给我听。如果你拉得很好，你可以继续上小提琴课，要是你拉得很差，你就不要再学了。"
"行。爸爸，"莎拉说，"这很公平。"
他很快就找到了一个好的小提琴老师，莎拉就开始学拉提琴了。尽管学费很高，但她爸爸遵守了诺言。
六个星期很快就过去了。莎拉该拉提琴给爸爸听了。
她走进起居室说："我准备好拉琴给你听了。"
"好哇，莎拉，"她爸爸说。"开始吧。"

她开始拉琴。她拉得很差，发出了可怕的噪音。她爸爸身旁有位朋友，朋友用手捂住了耳朵。

莎拉拉完一曲，她父亲说：“拉得好，莎拉。你可以继续学琴了。”

莎拉高兴地跑出门去。她父亲的朋友说：“你已经花了不少钱了，但她还是拉得很差。”

“噢，的确如此，”她爸爸说，“但自从她开始学小提琴，我就可以很便宜地买下这幢楼的五套房子了。再过六周，我就可以拥有整幢楼啦！”

★★★★★

I'll go there myself

There was once a **landlord** who always pretended he was **knowledgeable** though he was completely unable to read or write.

One day when the landlord was chatting with his guests, a servant came in and gave him a letter which asked him to lend a cow. The landlord was afraid that his guests would know he was unable to read or write, so he opened the envelope and glanced over the words. Then he said to the servant, “OK, please tell him I'll go there myself in a few minutes.”

我自己去那儿

从前，有一个地主是个既不会读也不会写的文盲，但他却偏要在人前装作很有学问。一天，当地主正和宾客聊天的时候，仆人走进来递给他一封信，信上说有人想向他借一头牛。地主害怕被客人知道自己是个文盲，于是他打开信封，瞧了瞧信上的字，然后对仆人说：“好的，你告诉他我马上自己去那儿。”

★★★★★

Why didn't you go with him？

When I was in the grocery store I heard my friend **moan**，“Oh，did I just make a **faux pas** ！” I stopped **thumping** melons and gave her my full attention.

“I ran into Mrs. Jones，” she wailed. “I didn't know that her husband died last week，and I asked her how he was feeling. She said，‘He's gone.’ I assumed he went someplace for his health，and I said...”

The words seemed to stick in her throat.

“What did you say？” I **prodded** her. “Good **riddance**？”

“Worse than that. I said，‘Why didn't you go with him？’”

你为什么不跟他一起去呢?

在杂货店里我听见我的朋友呻吟着说:“噢，我刚才不是冒犯人家了吗!”我停止拍打甜瓜，全神贯注地听她讲。

“我碰见了琼斯太太,”她哀号着。“我不知道她丈夫上周去逝了，我问她他身体怎么样。她说:‘他去了。’我以为他因为健康原因去了什么地方，我说……”

话似乎噎在了她的喉咙口。

“你说什么了?”我催促她，“死了倒干净?”

“比那还糟呢。我是说‘你为什么不陪他一起去呢?’”

实战提升 Practising & Exercise

单词 & 词组

keep one's promise 遵守诺言

well done 做得不错

landlord ['lændlɔːd] *n.* 房东，地主，（旅馆等的）老板

knowledgeable ['nɔlidʒəbl] *adj.* 知识渊博的，有见识的

moan [məun] *n.* 呻吟，哀悼，呼啸

faux pas [fəʊ'pɑː] *n.* 失礼，失言

thump [θʌmp] *v.* 重击，砰然地响

prod [prɔd] *v.* 刺

riddance ['ridəns] *n.* 摆脱，除去，驱逐，解除

知道不知道

各类乐器名一览

Clarinet 单簧管

Flute 长笛

Saxophone 萨克斯风

French Horn 法国号

Trumpet 小号

Viola 中提琴

Cello 大提琴

Guitar 吉他

Violin 小提琴

Harp 竖琴

Acoustic Grand Piano/Grand Piano 三角钢琴（用于演奏厅）

Garfield's Words
加菲猫语录精选

◎ Money is not everything. There's Master Card & Visa.
钞票不是万能的，有时还需要信用卡。

◎ One should love animals. They are so **tasty**.
每个人都应该热爱动物，因为它们很好吃。

◎ Save water. **Shower** with your girlfriend.
要节约用水，尽量和女友一起洗澡。

◎ Love the neighbor. But don't **get caught**.
要用心去爱你的邻居，不过不要让她的老公知道。

◎ Behind every successful man，there is a woman. And behind every unsuccessful man，there are two.
每个成功男人的背后，都有一个女人。每个不成功男人的背后，都有两个。

◎ Every man should marry. After all，happiness is not the only thing in life.
每个人都应该结婚。毕竟，快乐不是生命中唯一要追寻的东西。

◎ The wise never marry, and when they marry they become otherwise.

聪明人都不结婚，结婚的人很难再聪明起来。

◎ Success is a relative term. It brings so many relatives.

成功是一个相关名词，他会给你带来很多不相关的亲戚（联系）。

◎ Never put off the work till tomorrow what you can put off today.

不要等明天交不上差再找借口，今天就要找好。

◎ Love is **photogenic**. It needs darkness to develop.

爱情就象照片，需要大量的暗房时间来培养。

◎ Children in backseats cause accidents. Accidents in backseats cause children.

后排座位上的小孩会生出意外，后排座位上的意外会生出小孩。

◎ Your future depends on your dreams. So go to sleep.

现在的梦想决定着你的将来，所以还是再睡一会吧。

◎ There should be a better way to start a day than waking up every morning.

应该有更好的方式开始新一天，而不是千篇一律的在每个上午都醒来。

◎ Hard work never killed anybody. But why **take the risk**?

努力工作不会累死人！不过干吗要冒险证明呢?

◎ Work **fascinates** me. I can look at it for hours!

工作好有意思哦！尤其是看着别人工作。

◎ God made relatives；Thank God we can choose our friends.

神决定了谁是你的亲戚，幸运的是在选择朋友方面他给你留了余地。

◎ When two's company，three's the result!

两人作伴，三人为家！

◎ A dress is like a **barbed** fence. It protects the **premises** without **restricting** the view.

服饰就象铁丝网，它阻止你冒然行动但并不妨碍你尽情的观看。

◎ The more you learn，the more you know，the more you know，and the more you forget. The more you forget，the less you know. So why bother to learn ?

学的越多，知道的越多，知道的越多，忘记的越多，忘记的越多，知道的越少，为什么学来着?

实战提升

Practising & Exercise

单词 & 词组

tasty ['teisti] *adj.* 好吃的，可口的

shower ['ʃauə] *n.* 阵雨，淋浴

get caught 陷入

photogenic [ˌfəutəu'dʒenik] *n.* 适于拍照的；上照的

take the risk 冒险

fascinate ['fæsineit] *vt.* 使着迷，使神魂颠倒

barb [bɑ:b] *n.* 鱼钩，*vt.* 装倒钩于

premise ['premis] *vt.* 前提

restrict [ris'trikt] *vt.* 限制，约束

知道不知道

《加菲猫》(Garfield) 是一部美国连载漫画系列，由吉姆·戴维斯创作。加菲是一只橙色的、爱说风凉话、贪睡午觉、牛饮咖啡、大嚼千层面、见蜘蛛就扁、见邮差就穷追猛打的自信胖猫。他的名字取自吉姆·戴维斯的祖父詹姆斯·加菲尔·戴维斯 (James Garfield Davis)。吉姆·戴维斯是这样评价他的："大家爱加菲猫是因为它说出来的话与做出来的事人们也想说，也想做，却办不到。" 加菲猫的现实原型是异国短毛猫中的红虎斑异短。

Life after death
死后重生

Fresh milk

Customer：I wonder if this milk is **fresh**.

Waiter：Fresh？ Three hours ago it was grass.

新鲜牛奶

客户：我想知道这牛奶是否新鲜。

侍者：新鲜？三个小时以前它还是草。

★★★★★

Life after death

"Do you believe in life after death?" the boss asked one of his employees.

"Yes，Sir." the new **recruit** replied.

"Well，then，that makes everything just fine，" the boss went on. "After you left early today to go to your grandmother's funeral，she stopped in to see you.

死后重生

"你相信人死后仍有生命吗？" 老板问他的一个员工。

“是的，先生。”这个新员工回答说。
“哦，那么，这样说来一切就很正常了，”老板继续说，“在你今早离开去参加你奶奶葬礼后，她来看你了。”

★★★★★

How did you ever get here

One winter morning，an employee explained why he had shown up for work 45 minutes late. “It was so **slippery** out that for every step I took ahead，I slipped back two.”
The boss eyed him **suspiciously**. “Oh，yeah？ Then how did you ever get here？”
“I finally gave up,” he said，“and started for home.”

你是怎样来的?

一个冬天的早晨，一位员工向老板解释他为什么迟到了四十五分钟。“外面太滑了，我每向前迈一步，就要向后退两步。”
老板狐疑地看着他。“噢，是吗？那你是怎么到这里来的？”
“后来我决定放弃，”他说，“然后我就往家里走。”

实战提升
Practising & Exercise

单词 & 词组

fresh [freʃ] *adj.* 新鲜的；无盐味的，淡的
recruit [ri'kru:t] *vt.* 招募；组建
slippery ['slipəri] *adj.* 滑的；不老实的
suspiciously [sə'spiʃəsli] *adv.* 怀疑地

知道不知道

有没有想起鲁迅先生的那句名言？The cow eats grass but gives milk.（牛吃的是草，挤出来的是奶。）关于 milk，还有其他很多有趣的例句。

You only find out who's been swimming naked when the tide goes out

只有退潮时，才知道谁在裸泳

To be polite

One day, Bill and Tom went to a restaurant for dinner. As soon as the waiter took out two **steaks**, Bill quickly picked out the bigger steak for himself.

Tom wasn't happy about that: "When are you going to learn to be polite?"

Bill: "If you had the chance to pick first, which one would you pick?"

Tom: "The smaller piece, of course."

Bill: "What are you **whining** about then? The smaller piece is what you want, right?"

学会礼貌

一天，比尔和汤姆去餐馆吃饭。当服务员端上两份牛排时，比尔飞快地为自己挑了比较大的那块。

汤姆对此很不开心："你什么时候能学会礼貌？"

比尔说："如果让你先拿，你会拿哪个？"

汤姆说："当然是小的那个。"
比尔："那你还抱怨什么？小的那个不就是你想要的，不是吗？"

★★★★★

某次英文考试中翻英：
1. 我穿上外套，却发现第一个扣子掉了。
2. 他听见电话铃响，就过去接了电话。
正确答案应为：
1.I put on my coat and found its first button was gone.
2.As soon as he heard the phone ringing，he went to pick it up.
但是某生的答案是：
1.——！
2.Hello？

★★★★★

老师在黑板上写了一句：Time is money，并让同学们翻译。
有名学生答道：汤姆是玛丽。

★★★★★

上初一的时候，英语老师让我们读课文，恰好是一段对话，于是叫了一男一女两个同学来读。
男：What time is it now？
女：It's nine.
男：Let's go to bed.
女：We go to bed at nine.
全班绝倒。

★★★★★

Skinny dipping

One day Jimmy went down to the pond for a dip, but before he could **dive in** he **spied** his teacher, Mrs. Smith, emerging from **nude** bathing. When Mrs. Smith saw Jimmy, she **grabbed** the nearest object – which happened to be an old wooden box – and held it in front of her.

"Young man, I know what you're thinking," she said.

"And I know what you're thinking," replied Jimmy. "You're thinking that box has a **bottom** on it!"

裸泳

有一天吉米去池塘游泳，但在他跃入水里前看到他的老师史密斯小姐正从裸泳中冒出头来。当史密斯小姐看到吉米时，她赶紧抓过离自己最近的一件东西——碰巧是一个旧的木盒子，挡在自己前面，对他说："年轻人，我知道你在想什么。""我也知道你在想什么，"吉米答道，"你一定以为这个盒子是有底的！"

实战提升
Practising & Exercise

单词 & 词组

steak [steik] *n.* 牛排，肉排
whin [(h)win] *n.* 荆豆；棘豆
skinning dipping 裸泳，也可说 nude swimming
dive in 头朝下跳入水中
spy [spai] *v.* 看见，发现；间谍
nude [nju:d] *adj.* 裸体；裸体的
grab [græb] *v.* 抓住，吸引
bottom ['bɔtəm] *n.* 底部；末尾；臀部

知道不知道

说到裸泳，股神巴菲特（Warren Buffett）有句经典名言“You only find out who's been swimming naked when the tide goes out.”（只有退潮时，才知道谁在裸泳），用来指只有去除非理性市场因素，才能看清哪些公司具有真正的投资价值，哪些公司只不过是投机炒作。

Roast pig
烤乳猪

It's always me

A father said to his sons："Tomorrow your mother is going to bake a pie. Who is going to eat it？"

The oldest son replied："Father，I'll eat it all！"

The father then said："Tomorrow I'm going to **butcher** a pig. Who is going to eat it？"

The same son answered："Father，I'll eat it all！"

The father added："Tomorrow，we are going to **plough** the field. Who is going to plough？"

The oldest son answered again："It's always me，always me. Now it's someone else's turn to **volunteer**！"

总是我

一位父亲对他的儿子们说："你们的妈妈明天要烙一张馅饼，谁要吃呢？"

大儿子说："爸爸，我要把它都吃了。"

父亲接着说："明天我要杀一头猪，谁要吃呢？"

又是大儿子说："爸爸，我要把它都吃了。"

父亲又说："明天我们要耕地，谁想耕地呢？"

大儿子再次回答道："总是我，总是我，这次还是让其他人来做吧。"

★★★★★

Coincidence

A woman was singing. One of the guests turned to a man by his side and **criticized** the singer.

"What a terrible voice!" he said. "Do you know who she is ? "

"Yes," was the answer. "She is my wife."

"Oh, I beg your pardon." The man said, "Of course her voice is not bad, but the song is very bad. I wonder who wrote that **awful** song."

"I did." was the answer.

巧合

一位女士正在唱歌。一位客人转身对他旁边的男士批评道：

"多难听的嗓音！"他说，"你知道她是谁吗？"

"知道，"男士回答，"她是我太太。"

"噢，请你原谅。"客人说，"当然，她的嗓音并不坏，但那歌实在太差了。我真好奇是谁写了这么烂的歌。"

"是我。"男士回答道。

★★★★★

Roast pig

A gentleman was invited for dinner. When he hurried there and sat down,he was happy to see a roast pig in front of his seat. "Not bad, I am next to the pig." But then he noticed the angry fat lady sitting next to him. He faked a smile and added: "Oh I am sorry, I meant the roasted one on the table."

烤乳猪

一位先生应邀去赴宴。当他匆忙入座后，发现自己的座位正对着乳猪，于是大为高兴地说："还不错，我坐在乳猪的旁边。"但就在那时他发现身旁的一位胖女士正怒目相视，他忙陪笑改口到："对不起，我说的是那只烤好的。"

实战提升 Practising & Exercise

单词 & 词组

butcher ['butʃə] *n.* 肉贩，屠夫

plough [plau] *v.* 犁，耕地

volunteer [vɔlən'tiə(r)] *n.* 志愿者

coincidence [kəu'insidəns] *n.* 巧合，巧事

criticize ['kritisaiz] *v.* 批评，指责

awful ['ɔːful] *adj.* 糟糕的，可怕的

知道不知道

电影《V字仇杀队里》里有一句台词是这样的：There are no coincidences. Only the illusion of coincidence.（这世上没有巧合，只有巧合的错觉。）

A letter for the girlfriend
致女朋友的一封信

A letter for the girlfriend

One day a young man was writing a letter to his girl friend who lived just a few miles away in a nearby town. Among other things, he was telling her how much he loved her and how **wonderful** he thought she was. The more he wrote the more **poetic** he became. Finally, he said that in order to be with her he would suffer the greatest difficulties, he would face the greatest dangers that anyone could imagine. In fact, to spend only one minute with her, he would climb the highest mountain in the world, he would swim across the widest river, he would enter the deepest forest and with his **bare** hands fight against the fiercest animals.

He finished the letter, signed his name, and then suddenly remembered that he had forgotten to mention something quite important. So, in a **postscript** below his name, he added: "By the way I'll be over to see you on Wednesday night—if it doesn't rain."

致女朋友的一封信

一天，一个年轻男子给住在离他几英里远的镇上的女朋友写信。除写了其他的事情外，他告诉她：他爱她有多深，他认为她有多好。他越写越富有诗意，最后，他写道，为了能和她在一起，他将克服最大的困难，他将面对人可想像的最大危险。事实上，只要能和她待上一分钟，他就会爬越世界上最高的山，游过最宽的河，赤手空拳进入最浓密的森林同最凶恶的野兽搏斗。

他写完信，签好名，突然，他想起忘了写一件挺重要的事。因此，他在信末签名后又补充道："顺便说一下，我将在星期三晚上去看你——如果不下雨的话。"

★★★★★

Present for girlfriend

At a jewelry store, a young man bought an expensive **locket** as a present for his girlfriend. "Shall I **engrave** her name on it？" the jeweler asked.

The customer thought for a moment, and then said, "No–engrave it 'To my one and only love'. That way, if we ever break up, I can use it again."

送给女友的礼物

在一家珠宝店里，一位年轻人买了一个贵重的小金盒作为送给女友的礼物。"要我把她的名字刻在上面吗？"珠宝商问道。

那名顾客想了一会儿，然后说道："不——在上面刻'给我唯一的爱'。这样，如果我们闹崩了，我还可以再用到它。"

★★★★★

Asking a question

During the computer class, the teacher **chastised** one boy for talking to the girl sitting behind him.

"I was just asking her a question," the boy said.

"If you have a question, ask me," the teacher replied.

"OK," the boy answered. "Do you want to go out with me Friday night?"

问问题

计算机课上，老师批评一个男生，因为他和后边的女生说话。

"我只不过问她一个问题。"男生说。

"如果你有问题，问我好了。"老师说道。

"那好吧，"这位男生说，"周五晚上你愿意和我出去吗？"

★★★★★

The Three Stages of Man

He believes in Santa Claus.

He doesn't believe in Santa Claus.

He is Santa Claus!

男性成长的三阶段

相信圣诞老人的存在。

不相信圣诞老人的存在。

自己是个圣诞老人

★★★★★

Jack fell off his bicycle and got hurt. A beautiful young nurse asked him to fill forms. Jack finished them and gave them back. "Anything else ?" The nurse asked. "Yes," Jack thinks for a while and said "I'm a **bachelor**."

杰克骑车摔伤，去医院治疗。一位年轻美貌的护士拿着表格让填。杰克填好后递上表格"还有什么漏填的？"护士问。"有！"杰克想了想说，"我是个单身汉。"

实战提升 Practising & Exercise

单词 & 词组

wonderful ['wʌndəful] *adj.* 令人愉快的；奇妙的；非凡的；美好的

poetic [pəu'etik] *adj.*（与）诗（有关）的，用于诗的

bare [bεə] *adj.* 赤裸的，光秃秃的

postscript ['pəustskript] *n.*（信末签名后的）附言，又及

locket ['lɔkit] *n.* 金属装饰小盒，（挂在项链下的保藏纪念品的贵重）金属小盒

engrave [in'greiv] *v.* 雕刻（文字，图案）

chastise [tʃæs'taiz] *vt.* 厉声训斥；严厉谴责

bachelor ['bætʃələ] *n.* 单身汉；学士（仅用于头衔或固定用法）

知道不知道

bachelor party 就是在男生结束单身生活之前，他的好友会为他举办的一场 party，让他正式告别单身生活。对应地，wedding shower，也称为 bridal shower，指的则是女子婚前派对，是为即将结婚的女性举行的聚会。类似的表达还有 baby shower。Baby Shower 是美国的一项传统，是为即将生产的妈妈举办的"送礼聚会"，一方面向准妈妈表示祝贺，一方面也对准父母在经济上给予支持，一般在预产期前四到八周举办。送养育婴儿的必需品是聚会的核心内容。为了客人买礼物方便，在组织聚会时，主人会事先通知客人送礼的"主题"。例如，指定不同客人买适合婴儿在不同季节的用品，叫做"季节送礼会"(Seasonal Shower)，如果要求所有客人都送一包尿片，就叫做"尿片送礼会"(Diaper Shower)。主题完全根据需要设计，没有一定之规。

What I want in a man at different ages
我在不同年龄时的理想男友的标准

Original List (age 22)

1. Handsome
2. Charming
3. Financially successful
4. A caring listener
5. Witty
6. In good shape
7. Dresses with style
8. Appreciates finer things
9. Full of thoughtful surprises
10. An imaginative，romantic lover

原版（22 岁时）

1. 英俊
2. 有魅力
3. 有经济实力
4. 善于倾听
5. 机智
6. 良好的外形
7. 衣着有品味

8. 欣赏美好事物
9. 总有各种各样的惊喜
10. 富有想象力的浪漫情人

★★★★★

Revised List (age 32)

1. Nice looking (prefer hair on his head)
2. Opens car doors, holds chairs
3. Has enough money for a nice dinner
4. Listens more than talks
5. Laughs at my jokes
6. Carries bags of groceries with ease
7. Owns at least one tie
8. Appreciates a good home-cooked meal
9. Remembers birthdays and **anniversaries**
10. Seeks romance at least once a week

修订版（32 岁时）

1. 五官端正（有头发者优先）
2. 上车帮我开车门，入座帮我拉椅子
3. 有足够的钱享用美妙的晚餐
4. 少说多听
5. 我说笑话的时候一定要大笑
6. 逛街的时候帮我拎包
7. 至少有一条领带
8. 喜欢家里烹饪的晚餐
9. 记得我的生日和各个纪念日
10. 一周至少制造一次浪漫

★★★★★

Revised List (age 42)

1. Not too ugly (bald head OK)
2. Doesn't drive off until I'm in the car
3. Works steady—**splurges** on dinner out occasionally
4. Nods head when I'm talking
5. Usually remembers **punch** lines of jokes
6. Is in good enough shape to rearrange the furniture
7. Wears a shirt that covers his stomach
8. Knows not to buy champagne with **screw-top lids**
9. Remembers to put the toilet seat down
10. Shaves most weekends

修订版（42 岁时）

1. 不太丑（秃顶也可）
2. 我上车后才开车
3. 工作稳定——偶尔外出吃饭
4. 当我说话的时候点头
5. 通常记得笑话中的妙语
6. 有足够的力气搬家具
7. 没有啤酒肚
8. 懂得不买带螺旋盖的香槟
9. 记得放下马桶座圈
10. 大多数周末会刮胡子

★★★★★

Revised List (age 52)

1. Keeps hair in nose and ears **trimmed**
2. Doesn't **belch** or **scratch** in public
3. Doesn't borrow money too often
4. Doesn't nod off to sleep when I'm **venting**

5. Doesn't re-tell the same joke too many times
6. Is in good enough shape to get off couch on weekends
7. Usually wears matching socks and fresh **underwear**
8. Appreciates a good TV dinner
9. Remembers my name on occasion
10. Shaves some weekends

修订版（52 岁时）

1. 保持鼻子和耳朵处的毛发整洁
2. 不在公共场合打嗝或搔痒
3. 向别人借钱不要太频繁
4. 当我生气的时候不许打盹睡着
5. 不会多次重复讲同一个笑话
6. 周末不会一直赖在床上
7. 常换内衣裤，袜子要成对
8. 欣赏电视晚餐
9. 必要时记得我的名字
10. 有时周末会刮胡子

★★★★★

Revised List (age 62)

1. Doesn't scare small children
2. Remembers where bathroom is
3. Doesn't require much money for **upkeep**
4. Only **snores** lightly when asleep
5. Remembers why he's laughing
6. Is in good enough shape to stand up by himself
7. Usually wears clothes
8. Likes soft foods
9. Remembers where he left his teeth

10. Remembers that it's the weekend

修订版（62 岁时）

1. 不要吓唬小孩子
2. 记得浴室在哪
3. 不需要太多钱生活
4. 睡着的时候鼾声较小
5. 记得自己为何大笑
6. 行动自如
7. 通常穿着衣服
8. 喜欢软的食物
9. 记得把自己的假牙放哪了
10. 记得哪天是周末

★★★★★

Revised List (age 72)

1. Breathing
2. Doesn't miss the toilet

修订版（72 岁时）

1. 活的
2. 能找到洗手间

实战提升
Practising & Exercise

单词 & 词组

splurge [splə:dʒ] *vt.* 挥霍，大手大脚的花钱
punch [pʌntʃ] *n.* 猛击，推
witty ['witi] *adj.* 富于机智的，诙谐的
anniversary [,æni'və:səri] *n.* 周年纪念
screw-top lid，螺旋盖。从前，葡萄酒和香槟酒大都用橡木塞封装，但现在越来越多的酒商开始用螺旋盖代替橡木塞，本文中，螺旋盖被看做是廉价酒的“代名词”。
upkeep ['ʌpki:p] *n.* 维修（费），保养费；生活费
trim [trim] *vt.* 修剪，削减
belch [beltʃ] *v.* 打嗝，（火山、炮等）冒烟、喷出
scratch [skrætʃ] *n.* 刮，擦
vent [vent] *n.* 通风孔，烟道，火山口
underwear ['ʌndəwεə] *n.* 内衣
snore [snɔ:] *n.* 打鼾

知道不知道

如何形容魅力男人

He is so cute. 他很可爱。
Technically speaking，he is not my prince charming. 理论上来说，他还不是我的白马王子。
I had a feeling that he is the Mr. Right I was looking for. 我有一种感觉他就是我要找的那个男人。
He is one of the kind. 他是独一无二的。
He is an alpha male. 他是男人中的男人。

A Man vs. A Woman
男人和女人

A Man vs. A Woman

A woman **worries about** the future until she gets a husband. A man never worries about the future until he gets a wife.

男人和女人

女人总是担心将来，直到找到丈夫；男人从来不担心将来，直到有了妻子。

★★★★★

Successful Man and Woman

A successful man is one who makes more money than his wife can spend. A successful woman is one who can find such a man.

成功的男人和女人

成功的男人就是挣的钱比太太花的还多；成功的女人就是要能找到这样的男人。

★★★★★

Happy Man and Woman

To be happy with a man you must understand him a lot and love him a little. To be happy with a woman you must love her a lot and not try to understand her at all.

快乐的男人和女人

要和一个男人在一起很开心，就是要非常理解他，而只要爱他一点点；要和一个女人在一起很开心，就是必须要非常爱她，而决不要想法理解她。

★★★★★

A man will pay $2 for a $1 **item** he wants. A woman will pay $1 for a $2 item that she doesn't want.

男人需要的东西，虽然只值一块钱，也肯花两块钱去买；两块钱的东西降价到一块钱，女人虽然不需要，也会去买。

实战提升

Practising & Exercise

单词 & 词组

worry about 担忧，烦恼

item [ə'aitem] *n.* 条，项；项目；条款

知道不知道

有关 woman 的短语和习语

(one's) own woman 在判断或行动上独立的女人

a man of a woman 像男人的女人

comes the hours，comes the woman. 来得好不如来得巧。

She has always been her own woman. 她一向很独立。

all the old women of both sexes 婆婆妈妈的男人和女人

make an honest woman of sb. 和某人正式结婚

play the woman 撒娇；作女儿态（如哭泣、胆怯等）

kept woman 外室，靠男人养活的姘妇

necessary woman 女佣人，女仆

society woman 上流社会的妇女

woman of quality 贵妇，名媛

Mind twisters
脑筋急转弯

脑筋急转弯（一）

1. What will you break once you say it ?
什么东西一说出来就打破?

2. Will liars be honest after they die ?
骗子死了之后会诚实吗?

3. What always goes up and never goes down ?
什么东西只升不降?

4. Why did the boy make his dog sit in the sun ?
男孩为什么让他的狗坐在阳光下?

5. Why can a bride hide nothing ?
为什么新娘子什么也藏不住?

6. Why is the library the highest building ?
为什么图书馆是最高的建筑物?

7. What is the smallest bridge in the world ?
世界上最小的桥是什么?

8. What is the difference between the North Pole and the South Pole?
北极与南极的区别是什么?

9. What makes naughty boys long to work in a clock factory?
淘气的男孩为什么想去钟表厂工作?

10. What bird lifts heavy things?
什么鸟能举起重物?

11. A ship can contain only fifty persons. Now there is already forty–nine persons in it. At this time, a pregnant woman comes on and boards the ship. The ship sinks.Why?
有一艘船只能容纳 50 人，现在已有 49 人。这时一位孕妇上了船，船就沉了。为什么?

12. Why is the comet like Micky Mouse?
为什么是慧星像米老老鼠?

13. Who is closer to you, your mom or your dad?
谁跟你比较亲密，你的妈妈还是爸爸?

14. What's the poorest bank in the world?
世界上最贫穷的银行是什么?

15. What month do soldiers hate?
军人憎恨哪个月?

keys:

1. Silence.
沉默。

2. No，they won't. They lie still after they die.

不会，他们依旧撒谎。Lie still 躺着不动，依旧撒谎。

3. Your age.

你的年龄。

4. He wants to have a hot dog.

他想要一条热狗。

5. Because someone will give her away.

因为有人会揭发她。Give away 揭发，另有层意思是指在婚礼上把新娘交给新郎。

6. It has the most stories.

它的楼层最多。Story 故事，楼层。

7. The bridge of a nose.

鼻梁。

8. A whole world.

整个世界。 a world of difference 天壤之别。

9. They want to make faces.

make face 做鬼脸，做钟表面。

10. Crane.

鹤。Crane 鹤，举重机。

11. Because it is a pigbot.

那是潜水艇。pigbot，潜水艇。

12. Because it is a star with a tail.
因为它尾部有一个星。

13. Mom is closer，because Dad is father（farther）.
因为爸爸是父亲（更远的），所以妈妈比较靠近。

14. The river bank.
河岸。

15. March.
行军。

脑筋急转弯（二）

1. How many feet are there in a yard？
   院子里有几只脚?

2. Why is an empty purse always the same？
   为什么说空钱包总是相同的?

3. What kind of dog doesn't bite or bark？
   什么狗既不咬也不叫?

4. What is the smallest room in the world？
   世界上最小的房间是什么?

5. What kind of water should people drink in order to be healthy？
   为了健康，人们该喝什么水?

6. How do we know the ocean is friendly？
   我们怎么知道大海是友好的?

7. Which can move faster，heat or cold？
   热和冷，哪个跑的更快?

8. Why is the library the highest building？
   为什么图书馆是最高的建筑?

Keys:

1. It depends on how many people stand in the yard.
   要看有多少人站在院子里。yard 码，院子。

2. There is no change in it.
   因为它里面没有变化。change 零钱，变化。

3. Hot dog.

热狗。

4. Mushroom.

蘑菇。

5. Drink well water.

喝井水。well 井，健康的。

6. It waves.

它会招手。wave 起波浪，招手致意。

7. Heat，because you can catch cold.

热，因为你可以追上冷。catch cold 追上冷，患感冒。

8. It has the most stories.

因为它有最多的楼层。story 故事，层。

脑筋急转弯（三）

1. What fruit is never found singly ?
   什么水果永远不会是单个的?

2. Why are young men unwilling to date the daughter of the Fortunes ?
   年轻人为什么不愿意和福琼家女儿约会?

3. Why is an empty matchbox the best thing to have in the world ?
   为什么空火柴盒是世界上最好的东西?

4. Why did little Tom put his brother's guitar in the refrigerator ?
   小汤姆为什么把哥哥的吉他放在冰箱里?

5. What stays hot even if you tput it in a fridge ?
   什么东西即使放在冰箱里也热?

6. What kind of table has no legs ?
   什么桌子没有腿?

7. Why is a peacock the best story teller ?
   为什么孔雀最会讲故事?

8. Why does time fly ?
   时间为什么要飞?

9. What eight-letter word has only one letter in it ?
   哪个单词由 8 个字母组成，里面能装一封信。

10.What word is pronounced wrong，even by the best of scholars？

有个词，即使是最棒的学者也一定会念错。

11. Where does harvest come before work？

得在什么地方，收获会跑到劳动前面?

12. Why is the letter E so important？

字母 E 为什么这么重要?

keys：

采用了同音词（homonyms）：

1.A pear.（梨）

“pear”（梨）音同“pair”（一对）

2.Because she is Miss Fortune.（因为她是“不幸”小姐。）

Miss Fortune”音同“misfortune”（不幸）

运用了双关语（puns）:

3. Because it is matchless.（因为举世无双。）

“matchless”既可理解为“没有火柴的”，又可理解为“举世无双的，无可匹敌的”。

4. Because he enjoyed cool music.（因为他喜欢流行音乐。）

“cool”可表示“冷的、凉的”，也可指“棒、时髦、美妙的”。

5. Pepper.（辣椒。）

“hot”有两个意思：“热”、“辣”。

6. A timetable.

时间表，日程表。

7. Because it always has a beautiful tail.
因为它有漂亮的结尾。tail 结尾，尾巴。

8. Because many people are trying to kill it.
因为许多人都想消磨时光。kill 杀，消磨。

9. Envelope
信封。

10. The word “wrong” .
单词 wrong。

11. In a dictionary.
在字典里。

12. Because it is the beginning of everything.
因为它是万物的开始。

脑筋急转弯（四）

1. Where does afternoon come before morning in the world ?
   世界上什么地方下午在上午之前?

2. Why don't you take the bus home ?
   你为什么不乘公交车回家?

3. Why are the letter G and letter S in "gloves" close to each other ?
   在"gloves"一词中为什么说 g 和 s 紧紧相依?

4. What letter is an animal ?
   哪个字母是动物?

5. What letter is a question ?
   哪个字母是问题?

6. How do you feel today ?
   你今天感觉如何?

7. How can you make a rope shorter without cutting or winding it ?
   在不切断或缠绕的情况下，如何把一根绳子变短?

8. What can you tell from Peter's record card with extremely poor grades ?
   彼得的分数这么低，你怎么看?

9. What does everybody do at the same time ?
   所有人同时在做什么?

10. Who works only one day in a year but never gets fired？
谁一年只上一天班却不会被开除?

11. Why does the Statue of Liberty stand in New York harbour？
自由女神为何矗立在纽约港湾?

12. When can you go as fast as a racing car？
什么时候你能像跑车一样快?

keys：

1. In the dictionary.
字典里。

2. Because my home is not that big.
因为我家没那么大。take 乘坐，带着。

3. Because there is love between them!
因为它们之间有爱!

4. It's the letter B!
字母 B，bee 蜜蜂。

5. It's the letter Y.
字母 Y，why 为什么。

6. With my hands，of course!
当然用手啦!

7. Take a longer rope and compare with it!
拿一根更长的绳子和它比!

8. He didn't cheat!
他没有撒谎。

9. Grow old!
长大!

10. Santa Claus.
圣诞老人。

11. Because it can't sit down.
因为它不能坐下。

12. When you're in it.
当你坐在跑车里时。

脑筋急转弯（五）

1. Why are giraffes the cheapest to feed？
   为什么养长颈鹿最不花钱?

2. Why are dogs afraid to sunbathe？
   狗为什么害怕日光浴?

3. Why is the pig always eating？
   猪为什么没完没了地吃?

4. Why are politicians no longer concerned with snowball fights？
   政客们为什么不再关注打雪仗了?

5. Why don't women get bald as soon as men？
   为什么总是男人比女人先秃顶?

6. What can pierce ones ears without a hole？
   什么东西不用打洞就可以在耳朵上穿孔?

7. What is the longest word in the world？
   世界上最长的单词是什么?

8. Why does time fly？
   时间为何飞逝?

9. Where can a dog get another tail？
   狗去哪里可以再弄到一条尾巴?

10. If you drop a white hat into the Red Sea，what does it become？
    如果你往红海里丢一顶白帽子，它会变成什么样?

11. Who earns a living by driving his customers away？
谁通过把顾客赶走来谋生?

12. What starts with E，ends with E and only has one letter？
什么东西开头为 E，结尾也为 E，中间只有一个字母?

Keys：

1. They make a little food go a long way.
因为它们脖子长，一点点食物都要走很长的路才能咽下去。

2. They don't want to be hot-dog.
因为它们不想成为热狗。

3. Hes making a hog of himself.
它想成为一只肉猪。

4. The cold war is over.
冷战结束了。

5. Because women wear hair longer.
因为女人头发留得长。

6. Noise.
噪音。

7. Smiles. Because there is a mile between the letters.
微笑。因为两个字母 S 中间隔了一里。

8. To get away from all those who are trying to kill it.
为的是甩掉所有要谋杀它的人。

9. At a retail store.
在零售商店。

10. Wet
变湿了。

11. Taxi driver .
出租车司机。

12. An envelope.
信封。

脑筋急转弯（六）

1. Why are girls afraid of the letter C？

   女孩为何害怕字母 C？

2. Why is U the jolliest letter？

   为什么 U 是最快乐的字母?

3. Why do lions eat raw meat？

   狮子为什么吃生肉?

4. How many sides does a circle have？

   圆有几个面?

5. Where was the Declaration of Independence signed？

   独立宣言是在哪里签署的?

6. If two's company and three's crowd，what's four and five？

   如果二是同伴，三是人群，四和五是什么?

7. The farmers in this village used modern methods but harvested no apples this year，why？

   有个村庄的农民，今年用了现代方法，但没收获到苹果，为什么?

8. Lucky Mouse fell off a 1000-step stair and was not hurt. why？

   有只幸运的老鼠从1000层的楼梯上摔下来却没受伤，为什么?

9. How can you make 6 out of three 7's？

   如何用三个 7 得到 6？

10. How can you make 6 out of three 5's ?

三个 5 如何得出 6 ?

11. how can you make 1000 out of eight 8's ?

八个 8 如何得出 1000 ?

12. How do you know policemen are strong ?

你怎么知道警察强壮?

13. What must you do before you return a book to the library ?

在你给图书馆还书前，你必须做什么?

Keys:

1. Because it makes fat fact!

因为它让肥胖变成事实!

2. Because it's in the midst of fun!

因为它在 fun 的中间!

3. They don't know how to cook!

他们不知道如何烹饪！

4. Two. The inside and the outside!

两个，里面和外面!

5. At the bottom!

在末尾!

6. Nine!

9！

7. They planted peach trees!

他们种的是桃子！

8. He fell off the last step!

他从最后一级台阶摔下来！

9.easy . 7− 7/7=6!

简单，7− 7/7=6!

10. easy. 5+5/5=6!

简单，5+5/5=6!

11. easy. 8+8+8+88+888=1000!

简单，8+8+8+88+888=1000!

12.Because they can hold up traffic with just one hand!

因为他们只用一只手就能控制交通了！

13.Borrow the book from library.

借书。

脑筋急转弯（七）

1. Why are people tired on April Fool's Day ?
   愚人节人们为什么疲倦?

2. What weather do mice and rats fear ?
   老鼠害怕什么天气?

3. When do dogs refuse to follow their masters ?
   狗什么时候不愿跟随主人?

4. What question can never be answered by "yes" ?
   哪个问题永远不能回答"是的"？

5. What tree is always very sad ?
   什么树总是很伤心?

6. When can you get water with a net ?
   什么时候可以用网兜装水?

9. What question is that to which you must always answer "yes" ?
   什么问题你只能回答"yes"？

10. Where were you when the power was cut off ?
    停电的时候你在哪?

11. When is a blue book not a blue book?
    蓝书什么时候不蓝?

12. Why is a calendar so popular ?
    月历为何这么受欢迎?

13. What key can't open a door ?

提示 : 这个单词包含字母 key，是一种动物

Keys:

1. Because they have just had a long March.

因为他们刚过了长长的三月。March 三月 ; 行军。

2. When it's raining cats and dogs.

下大雨。rain cats and dogs 下大雨。

3. When their masters go to the flea market.

主人去跳蚤市场时。Flea 跳蚤，flea market 旧货市场。

4. Are you asleep ?

你睡着了吗?

5. Weeping willow.

垂柳。 weep 哭泣 ; willow 柳树。

6. When water is turned into ice.

当水结成冰时。

9 . "What does y–e–s spell ? "

(当别人问你) "yes" 怎么拼?

10. In the darkness.

在黑暗中。

11. When the book is red.

与 read 同音 。

12. Because it has a lot of dates.

因为它里面有很多约会。date 日子、约会。

13. Monkey.

猴子。